Toxicity in the Workplace

Toxicity
in the
Workplace

*Coping with Difficult
People on the Job*

Shonda Lackey, PhD

**ROCKRIDGE
PRESS**

Interior and Cover Designer: Rachel Haeseker
Art Producer: Tom Hood
Editor: Nora Spiegel
Production Editor: Ruth Sakata Corley

ISBN: Print 978-1-64611-463-4 | eBook 978-1-64611-464-1
R0

Contents

Introduction vi

Chapter 1:
Understanding Difficult Coworkers and Toxic Behavior 1

Chapter 2:
Needs Constant Reassurance 35

Chapter 3:
Can't Focus on Tasks 49

Chapter 4:
Struggles with Follow-Through 63

Chapter 5:
Says One Thing but Does Another 77

Chapter 6:
All Ego, All the Time 91

Chapter 7:
More Workplace Difficulties 105

Chapter 8:
Conclusion 125

Resources 133
References 135
Index 138

Introduction

Are you fed up with the way some of your coworkers treat you and maybe even wondering if you should quit your job because you just can't take any more of your toxic workplace? Do you feel alone, as if you're the only person in your office who sees what's really happening? Spending many hours in professional situations like this each week can make you feel stressed out, isolated, and trapped.

You may keep your concerns to yourself because you feel as if no one understands or cares about what you're going through. If you do speak up, you may fear that your friends, family, and other coworkers will tire of hearing you talk about your work problems. You may also suspect that they won't understand how frustrated you are, because they haven't had to face what you're up against in your daily work environment. This is especially true if the people you're close to have worked in generally supportive environments and believe their job gives them a sense of purpose. Perhaps they only deal with the typical stress of tight deadlines or minor conflicts with coworkers.

Chances are that you picked up this book because your workplace problems are more severe. Your colleagues may pass their work duties off to you, belittle you, stand over your shoulder to double-check your work, or dominate the office with passive-aggressive manipulation or angry outbursts.

Your family and friends may wonder why you can't just quit, but leaving a job is not always easy. The pressure of bills and other financial responsibilities, plus the process of starting over, can make it feel impossible to leave. Even the idea of searching for another job can be daunting. It's also difficult to consider leaving if you take satisfaction in the work you do. You may think that if anyone should leave the job or change their behavior, it should be your colleague, but difficult people rarely seem to leave jobs on their own or get fired for their behavior. In fact, they often seem to get bolder when their destructive actions go unchecked, and difficult colleagues may even seem to earn rewards for their behavior.

Does your difficult colleague get raises and promotions, while you only seem to get criticized despite working hard? Do the most seemingly problematic people in your workplace get recognition, while it doesn't come your way? Perhaps your boss or other colleagues appear to have a positive view of the coworker who treats you rudely. These dynamics are frustrating but unfortunately all too common. Over the years, many people in similar situations have come to me for help in figuring out how to work with difficult coworkers and function better in a toxic work environment. As a licensed clinical psychologist, I've helped several people who could not immediately quit their jobs and had to find a way to work with colleagues they considered difficult.

Aside from slowing down productivity, toxic workplace behaviors can lead some employees to experience depression, anxiety, and other psychological problems. Sometimes a workplace is negatively affected by the toxic behavior of employees struggling with untreated mental health problems. Yet workplaces are often unprepared to handle this range of health concerns in employees who exhibit toxic behaviors—and in their colleagues who struggle with this negativity. Talking about mental health issues may be taboo. People who affect others with their toxic behaviors may not want to disclose their personal issues. Others may not be aware of the impact of their behavior. Either way, you may be criticized for pointing out problems.

Many of the people I have treated sought help because they started to experience mental health problems like depression and anxiety as a result of their stressful work environment. Some of these people had never experienced mental health issues before. Others had a history of mental health problems that resurfaced because of the stress of working with people who behaved in dysfunctional ways. One of the most helpful things they learned was how to respond to their colleagues' behavior by being assertive in their communication and actions. Through therapy, they learned how to manage their emotions and to work around dysfunctional behavior. In cases where the workplace and colleagues proved resistant to change, many of the people I treated gained the confidence to execute an exit strategy and move on to healthier workplaces. I have also treated people who came to realize how their own dysfunctional behavior caused problems within their workplace. These people learned how to interact with their colleagues in a more compassionate and productive way.

This book is intended for people who have coworkers who are difficult to deal with because they may have a mental disorder. These coworkers may be your peers, your boss, or people you manage. This book is not a substitute for mental health treatment. If you are really struggling, please consult the resources section to locate a licensed mental health professional, such as a psychologist, for personalized help.

This book is also not intended to encourage you to diagnose your coworkers. Keep in mind that only a qualified mental health professional can diagnose someone with a mental disorder. However, being aware of the symptoms of a possible mental disorder may give you some insight into your coworker's behavior and prevent you from taking it personally. Dealing with toxic behaviors can be confusing and upsetting, but understanding the possible causes can help you gain clarity. Instead of getting frustrated or distracted by your colleague's actions, you can decrease your stress, gain peace of mind, and focus on producing quality work.

My hope is that this book will reassure you that you are not alone. My goal is to help you gain insight into the possible causes of your coworker's behavior and give you practical strategies you can use right away to help you deal with it. Although you can't control your coworker's behavior, you can improve your situation by learning how to change the way you respond to it.

Chapter 1

Understanding Difficult Coworkers and Toxic Behavior

This chapter will help you understand how mental health problems affect workplace productivity and relationships. When you understand the possible causes of a colleague's behavior, you'll be better equipped to handle your interactions with them. Common mental disorders covered include anxiety and mood, personality, and neurodevelopmental disorders. I'll also describe how the behavior of someone with any of these suspected mental disorders may lead to workplace problems. Finally, I'll share with you a summary of behavioral and communication techniques designed to decrease your stress and help you be more productive at work. You can use these techniques right away when interacting with your colleagues.

More Than a Personality Clash

No person or workplace is perfect. Even if you love your job and your work environment, you're bound to experience some conflict occasionally. You and your manager may have different ideas about the most effective way to get a job done. Maybe a coworker who is generally collaborative has a bad day and takes it out on you by making snappy comments. Perhaps tensions increase and tempers flare during high-stress periods when your team is driving hard to meet a deadline.

However, there is a difference between typical workplace conflict and difficulty getting along with someone who has a mental disorder. The key difference is that a colleague with a mental disorder tends to be more deeply set in their ways, which makes it more difficult to reason with them or negotiate an alternative way of interacting. Their behavior will likely be more extreme and resistant to change, yet they usually don't see their behavior as problematic. This is especially true when someone has a personality disorder such as narcissistic personality disorder (NPD), borderline personality disorder (BPD), or obsessive-compulsive personality disorder (OCPD).

For example, someone who isn't affected by a mental health problem may talk over you in a meeting. They may become so excited about an idea that they just can't hold back their input. It's also possible that they think you're taking too long to get to the point and they want to push the conversation along. If in this situation you let your colleague know that you don't like the way they are treating you, they will likely be mindful of your feelings and probably apologize. They will also probably recognize how their behavior could negatively affect your workplace and relationship and will be careful not to talk over you again.

Someone with a mental disorder may not think they are doing anything wrong if they talk over you. They may accuse you of being too sensitive or criticize the way you presented your idea. In this case, your colleague will probably not care about your feelings or make any attempt to change their behavior. In fact, they will probably talk over you at the next meeting, as if you had never addressed the issue with them.

People with mental disorders typically interact with people in a similar manner. They will probably behave the same way when interacting with their boss, peer, or a person they manage. In some cases, such as when a colleague might have NPD, you may see them dial back their behavior when interacting with people whom they perceive as powerful. But when your colleague has a mental disorder, their behavior typically has a consistent pattern that is resistant to your attempts to reach a resolution. If this person is a manager, the turnover rates of people they manage are usually high.

This book is for people who are trying their best to work with difficult colleagues but are being pushed to the limit. You may have a boss who keeps checking in on you to make sure you're completing tasks the way they prefer. They may flood your inbox or call you after hours asking for updates. You may manage a team member whose forgetful and sluggish behavior makes you anxious about meeting deadlines, or one who thinks they know it all and treats you in a condescending manner. Yet another colleague may pit you against another, causing team dynamics to break down. If you're getting worn out dealing with the way people act in your workplace and just can't seem to take any more, I hope that the tips in this book make your life less stressful.

Refrain from Diagnosing Your Coworker

Avoid informal diagnosing of a coworker's potential mental disorder. Only a qualified mental health professional can diagnose someone by conducting a full psychological assessment. No one else can be completely sure if a person has a mental disorder at all. There is also significant symptom overlap between some mental disorders, so without a true diagnosis, it is difficult to know what problems your colleague may be dealing with.

Trying to diagnose a coworker may make things worse. You may then struggle to see their humanity or pathologize all of their behavior as a symptom, discounting valid input. For example, if your colleague assertively disagrees with a business strategy, you may discount it as a symptom rather than consider their potentially useful insight.

Considering possible motivations for your colleague's behavior may decrease your frustration and stress. As you learn about what your colleague may be going through, you can refrain from labeling them, choose not to take their behavior personally, and consider the possibility that their behavior is influenced by problems with the way they perceive themselves and others.

Toxic Behavior vs. Toxic People

What comes to mind when you hear the word "toxic"? Maybe the first thing you think about is something unsafe and poisonous, like chemicals. Or maybe you think about workplace environments like those that have been exposed during recent scandals in various industries.

In some workplaces, dysfunctional behavior is harmful and can cause production and team dynamics to break down. This behavior can also spread throughout various departments and infect entire companies.

It can be tempting to call one of your colleagues toxic, but that's not always the most helpful approach. When we call another *person* toxic, it often makes our interactions with them worse. You both may feel hopeless that change can ever be possible. Your colleague may wonder how they can change something you've determined is a fundamental part of who they are. Calling a person toxic also makes it easier to ostracize them. Some of these people may have mental disorders; feeling stigmatized can make their problems more severe and make them even less likely to get help.

This book focuses on the toxic *behavior* of people at work. Focusing on your colleague's behavior means that specific things can be changed. Do they try to get you to do their work? Do they speak to you in a condescending or rude way? Are they usually late or unreliable on team projects? Focusing on behavior can also help you develop some empathy for your colleague's situation, while gaining the ability to assert yourself.

How This Book Can Help

You may have chosen this book because you're feeling stuck and overwhelmed due to all the challenges in your workplace. You may dread going into work and are just trying to figure out how much you can take before you quit. This is a very stressful situation and can seem impossible to fix.

So what can you do now? This book will give you comprehensive information about a variety of mental disorders that affect workplace behavior and treatment of coworkers, insight into how to understand your coworker's behavior, and tips for how to cope with it. I hope that you'll feel more confident and less stressed by putting these suggestions into practice.

This book has been tailored to people who have coworkers whose dysfunctional behavior may be explained by an untreated mental disorder. These coworkers may be your peers, your boss, or people you manage.

The information in this book is not a substitute for mental health treatment. Still, having knowledge of what it's like for someone to struggle with a possible mental disorder may decrease some of the resentment, anger, and stress you could be experiencing while working with your colleague. You will gain insight into your coworker's interpersonal style, as well as practical tips that work best with that specific style. You can't control how your coworker behaves, but you can choose how and where you want to focus your energy.

Overview of Common Mental Health Concerns

According to the *Diagnostic and Statistical Manual of Mental Disorders, Fifth Edition (DSM-5)*, a mental disorder involves a major problem with the way a person thinks, feels, and behaves. These impairments make it difficult to function socially and in other areas of life, such as work or school. The disorders listed here from each *DSM-5* category are those most likely to lead to destructive behavior in your workplace.

Anxiety Disorders

Individuals who suffer from anxiety disorders experience fear or worry so severe that it interferes with daily life.

→ **Generalized Anxiety Disorder:** Someone with this disorder exhibits worry about several major areas of life and often assumes the worst is going to happen. They may be restless, frustrated, tense, tired, and forgetful.

Someone at work who possibly has generalized anxiety disorder usually assumes the worst, so they may approach most situations as if they're a matter of life and death. These individuals may literally run back and forth nervously. They may also have memory problems due to poor concentration.

→ **Panic Disorder:** Someone with this disorder experiences panic attacks, which involve physiological symptoms such as sweating, heart palpitations, and shortness of breath. A person having a panic attack may also have a sense of dying or losing control, and they may feel as if they or their surroundings are not real.

Someone with panic disorder may exhibit sudden changes in breathing. They may appear as if they've blanked out and can seem disconnected from you. They may then need to excuse themselves from a meeting or a discussion to calm down.

→ **Social Phobia:** A person with social phobia has extreme anxiety about social interactions and fears being judged negatively. This individual typically avoids anxiety-inducing situations or shows up anyway with significant anxiety.

People with social phobia will usually avoid tasks that involve interacting with people, and they may have trouble speaking up in meetings. They may also avoid office parties or other social events and refrain from engaging in small talk.

You'll find more about how to interact with someone with a possible anxiety disorder in chapters 2, 3, 4, and 7.

Mood Disorders

Individuals who suffer from mood disorders experience frequent and significant fluctuations in their emotional state.

→ **Major Depressive Disorder:** Someone with this disorder may experience depressed mood, loss of interest in activities, weight loss or gain, lack of sleep or excessive sleep, and fatigue. They may feel worthless, move slowly, and have impaired memory. It is possible that they think about death or suicide or have planned to die by suicide.

Someone at work with possible major depressive disorder may be forgetful, unmotivated, and irritable. They may arrive late to work, call out sick frequently, and isolate themselves from others. They may speak and appear to move slowly. Major depressive disorder is particularly likely if a colleague previously performed at a high level and then a noticeable change in their demeanor and productivity occurred.

→ **Bipolar Disorder:** A person with bipolar disorder can be diagnosed with Bipolar I or Bipolar II. People with Bipolar I must have experienced a manic episode consisting of an elevated or irritable mood. Other symptoms of a manic episode include high self-esteem; decreased sleep; talkativeness; racing thoughts; difficulty concentrating; increased motivation and action toward social, work, school, or sexual goals; and involvement in high-risk activities. A major depressive episode may or may not occur. People with Bipolar II have never experienced a manic episode, but they have experienced hypomania (fewer manic symptoms for a lesser period than mania). They must also experience a major depressive episode, as described in the previous section.

Someone with possible bipolar disorder at work may show signs of depression, as described above. They may also show signs of mania or hypomania. These people may exhibit extreme shifts in productivity and in the quality of their work. They may be creative, productive, and charismatic for a period, then their mood may shift and cause them to be isolated, irritable, and unable to complete tasks.

You'll learn more about how to interact with someone with a possible mood disorder in chapters 3, 4, and 7.

Personality Disorders

A personality disorder is a long-standing pattern of rigid behavior in many different settings. This behavior diverges from cultural expectations and can affect an individual's thinking, feelings, social interactions, and impulse control.

→ **Narcissistic Personality Disorder (NPD):** An individual with NPD may think of themselves as superior or special. They may be manipulative, envious, and focused on success or power. Often, they need to be praised, act entitled, show off, and can't understand the feelings of others.

Someone at work with possible NPD might have a reputation for being a "know-it-all." They are quick to criticize and slow to offer praise. When they make mistakes, they don't take responsibility. They are often hostile and may have a menacing stare and an imposing stance. These individuals may ask personal questions so they can exploit their colleagues' weaknesses. They typically associate most with colleagues whom they consider powerful, while ignoring everyone else and using a condescending tone if they do speak to them. They use most opportunities to make themselves seem important by speaking about their achievements or social connections, and they must be the center of attention and dominate conversations by not letting anyone else speak. These individuals can become angry enough to yell at or threaten coworkers when they feel criticized. You'll find more about working with someone with possible NPD in chapters 5, 6, and 7.

→ **Borderline Personality Disorder (BPD):** An individual with BPD has a history of unstable relationships. They are sensitive to abandonment and often alternate between thinking the best and worst of someone. They can sometimes become paranoid and suspicious of others. Their self-image is also unstable, and they are often impulsive. Individuals with this disorder may attempt suicide or engage in self-mutilation. They can also experience sudden shifts in mood, as well as inappropriate anger.

Someone with possible BPD at work may have intense shifts in mood. They may act as if a coworker is their best friend, then be cold and distant with that person hours later. They will often sabotage the work of others to make their colleagues seem incompetent. Individuals with this disorder will often try to figure out a coworker's insecurities so they can use them to make that person feel less confident. They can get angry when they perceive rejection or receive criticism and may even perceive criticism when there is none. For example, someone with possible BPD might misinterpret the facial expression of a colleague who is deep in thought and think this person is upset with them. These individuals may also make their colleagues uncomfortable by invading their personal space or by sharing personal information about themselves. They often pit one coworker against another, resulting in devastating team dynamics. You'll find more about working with coworkers with possible BPD in chapters 5 and 7.

→ **Obsessive-Compulsive Personality Disorder (OCPD):** An individual with this disorder is driven by perfectionism. They are rigid in their thinking and set strict standards guided by details, rules, and lists. Rather than being productive, these standards often slow down the process involved in completing a task. They often demand things be done a certain way and may have difficulty assigning responsibility to others. Individuals with this disorder may sacrifice relationships with friends and family because of their commitment to work. They may not like spending money and may refuse to throw out things they no longer need.

Someone with possible OCPD at work may have a reputation for being a micromanager. These individuals may set unrealistic standards and be hesitant to delegate tasks. For example, they may ask a colleague to keep revising a presentation to the point where it puts them behind schedule. Individuals with this disorder are typically afraid to change workplace protocols, even if there are more effective ways of getting things done. They may appear well-organized and rely on checklists or color-coordinated systems. They may seem overly committed to work, rarely taking vacations or calling out sick. You'll find more about how to interact with someone with possible OCPD in chapter 7.

Neurodevelopmental Disorders

Individuals with neurodevelopmental disorders experience impairments in the way their brain and/or central nervous system develops, which can lead to problems with motor skills, learning, and communication.

→ **Attention-Deficit/Hyperactivity Disorder (ADHD):** An individual with this disorder may have symptoms of inattention and/or hyperactivity and impulsivity. One symptom of inattention is difficulty paying close attention—they may seem as if their mind is elsewhere when you're speaking to them. Other signs include not completing tasks, difficulty organizing, losing things that are needed to complete tasks, and avoiding situations in which they need to pay attention for a prolonged period. Symptoms of hyperactivity and impulsivity can include fidgeting, leaving seated positions, inappropriate running or climbing, difficulty carrying out actions quietly, talking a lot, interrupting others, and impatience.

Someone at work with possible ADHD may be hyperactive and impulsive. They may speak before they think and make insensitive comments. This person may also have difficulty waiting their turn and may interrupt other people in meetings. Due to their organizational problems they may be forgetful, have difficulty with time-management, and keep their work-space noticeably messy. Someone with ADHD may not seem to pay attention at work and may ask colleagues to repeat themselves several times. You'll find more about how to interact with someone with possible ADHD at work in chapters 3, 4, and 7.

By the Numbers

Stigma about mental disorders can cause some people to feel embarrassed and hesitant to seek treatment. People who fear that they may be ostracized may not talk about their mental health problems; they usually feel like they're alone in their experience.

Still, statistics show that anyone can suffer from a mental health problem at some point in their life. A National Alliance on Mental Illness (NAMI) study found that, in any given year, 19.1 percent of adults—or 47.6 million people in the United States—have a mental disorder. Among the conditions described in this chapter, 19.1 percent had an anxiety disorder diagnosis, followed by 7.2 percent with a major depressive episode, and 2.8 percent with bipolar disorder. The National Institute of Mental Health also reports that 4.4 percent of adults have ADHD.

It takes time before many people are willing or able to seek treatment for a mental illness. NAMI reports that, on average, 11 years pass between people first exhibiting symptoms and seeking treatment. People may lack awareness of a problem, have confusion about the process of seeking treatment, lack funds for services, or fear change.

Mental disorders affect people from all backgrounds, but with proper treatment, people can live productive lives. Researchers continue to identify evidence-based solutions that help improve the psychological health of people living with mental disorders.

Improving Your Work Situation

You may be unsure how to improve conditions at work caused by your colleague's toxic behavior. You may be surrounded by disgruntled employees with low morale or asked to take on more responsibilities due to high employee turnover. The office mood may be so bad that you can feel the tension as soon as you walk through the door. Although you may feel some empathy for your coworker's mental health problems, you may feel resentful or anxious as the stress of a toxic workplace continues to build.

Your first instinct may be to let resentment, anger, anxiety, or other negative feelings influence how you respond to your colleague. You may believe that others should behave a certain way, and it can be difficult to accept that their standards and values differ from yours. If this is so, you may find it helpful to focus on your preferences as yours alone and to let go of any expectations or demands on the way others behave. Holding on to rigid beliefs can cause negative feelings to fester.

Two people with similar backgrounds can be treated the same way in a toxic environment, with each interpreting the situation differently. One person might say, "She shouldn't behave like that. It's her fault this workplace is so toxic." The other might say, "I don't like her behavior and I'd prefer she not act like that, but nobody's perfect. I'm going to change what I can and see if it makes a difference."

Focusing on your own behavior can make you feel empowered by your ability to make a choice despite being in a situation that can make so many people feel powerless. Once you make the decision to adjust how you interact with colleagues, you may wonder how to make these changes. Your first attempt may be to change the way you behave and communicate with them. At the core of these boundary-setting techniques is assertiveness—the ability to confidently express your preferences and needs without being aggressive. Assertive communication and behavior are techniques you can use in many different situations throughout your life.

If you're in a management position, part of solving problems with your staff may involve offering them reasonable accommodations. According to the Americans with Disabilities Act of 1990, people in the United States with disabilities, including certain mental disorders, can be eligible to receive some flexibility at work if it doesn't disrupt the workplace flow. These changes to their job tasks or workplace are known as "reasonable accommodations."

As an example, one of your employees with depression may have difficulty waking up in time to get to the office at 9:00 a.m. A reasonable accommo-dation could be giving that employee a more flexible schedule, allowing them to arrive at 10:00 a.m. and stay until 6:00 p.m. instead of 5:00 p.m.

If you've done your best to resolve workplace issues directly with your colleague but can't reach a resolution, you may have to report the issue to some-one at a higher level of authority. In extreme cases, you may have to consider finding another job. This may seem unfair, but it is an option to consider so that you can protect your own well-being.

Mitigating Stress

According to the World Health Organization (WHO), toxic behavior in the workplace is associated with some people's experience of poor mental and physical health. Toxic environments—low support, rigid working hours, poorly defined roles, a lack of methods to voice concerns, and bad communica-tion and management—are likely to lead to poor mental health.

If you work in a toxic environment, you may expe-rience depression, anxiety, anger, insomnia, and other psychological problems, as well as physical symptoms such as muscle tension, headaches, and stomachaches. These symptoms can cause you to call out sick, or if you are able to show up, you may per-form poorly due to shaky morale and confidence.

Let's take a closer look at how damaging stressful workplaces can be to get a better understanding of their full impact. Stress is your body's reaction to a specific external trigger and typically ends when that trigger is removed. For example, if you have three presentations all due the same week, you may feel worried and even have muscle tension or headaches. However, these symptoms will usually disappear after your presentations are done.

Chronic stress can lead to anxiety—a fearful response to stress. For example, if you're in a chronically stressful work environment, you may fear you're going to be fired if you speak up. You may also worry about how long you can put up with the situation because you can't afford to quit right away.

One of the most damaging ways stress can affect you is by compromising your immune system. It can also make you vulnerable, increasing your chances of developing a mental disorder and/or exacerbating existing mental disorders. For some, workplace stress leads to poor relationships outside of work, as they may take frustrations out on friends and family and get into physical or verbal arguments with them. In some cases, people may abuse substances to deal with the stress caused by a toxic work environment.

There are healthy ways to combat this damaging workplace stress. One of the primary ways is setting boundaries. Does one of your colleagues contact you after hours with work-related questions? Set your voicemail and automated e-mail replies to indicate what hours you are available to review messages. Is there a person in your office you feel uncomfortable speaking to because they always ask personal questions? Let them know that you don't discuss those topics at work and that you feel uncomfortable doing so. Some benefits of enforcing healthy boundaries include less stress, better sleep, and increased self-esteem—improvements in health that may help you be more engaged at work.

Maintaining Productivity

Dealing with your coworker's difficult behavior can take a toll on your productivity. Leadership often sets the tone for your organizational culture and standards for acceptable behavior in your workplace. Certain negative behaviors from leadership can spread through the company and infect one coworker after the next.

The behaviors of your peers or people you manage could also have devastating results for the workplace. It may seem that nothing you do is ever good enough. You may have colleagues who are afraid to try more effective techniques or ones who can't meet deadlines. There might also be colleagues who think they know everything and refuse to listen to your feedback.

Productivity in the workplace thrives when employees are healthy and motivated. Toxic environments, on the other hand, create low morale and productivity. When you feel stuck in a toxic environment, you often don't see the point in putting in your best effort to produce quality work. You may call out sick and, even if you are present, do the bare minimum. This often happens to people who were once productive and present until they started to get beaten down by office politics. High turnover rates typically occur in offices like this, leaving the remaining employees to take on extra work. The added stress from an increased workload can also result in a work product that does not represent your true ability.

There are still ways to take control of your workplace situation, to maintain a high level of productivity, and to produce quality work. If you are a manager and notice morale is low, it may be helpful to acknowledge the situation and ask your employees for feedback about it. Perhaps your colleagues feel stressed because they're asked to do too much with too few resources. You can find ways to show you appreciate the work they do, both through verbal praise and tangible rewards.

Productivity in a toxic workplace, especially if you're not in a leadership position, may mean using certain behavioral and communication techniques to set boundaries. Even though there's only so much you can change on your own, at least you can acknowledge you're doing the best you can in the situation.

Why It Matters

In addition to the financial compensation work gives us, many people enjoy the sense of purpose they get from using their talents to help others solve problems. However, not everyone can be as productive and purposeful as they'd like to be at work. NAMI reports that, worldwide, depression is the main cause of disability that makes it challenging—and sometimes even impossible—to work.

Employees' mental health problems often result in monetary costs for employees and employers alike. WHO reports that workplace environments that contribute to mental health problems lead to decreased productivity and absenteeism. NAMI reports that each year in the United States, mental health issues result in a loss of earnings of $193.2 billion.

There are also costs to the quality of life for employees and the organizations where they work. Employees can experience a weakened immune system, inflammation, anxiety, depression, and other psychological problems. According to the American Psychiatric Association Foundation, chronic stress in the workplace can result in as many as 120,000 deaths per year.

Everyone benefits when companies play an active role in promoting the well-being of their employees. WHO defines a healthy workplace as one where employees and leadership work together to create an environment where the well-being of staff is valued. Workplace health has such a positive impact on the bottom line—as well as on employees' mental and physical health—that it is even more important for companies to understand how psychologically healthy workplaces benefit employees and the organization. The American Psychological Association Center for Organizational Excellence notes many benefits for employees, including improvements in morale, job satisfaction, health, motivation, and stress management. Organizations benefit from improvements in employee performance, productivity, attendance, safety, retention, and customer service.

Real-World Solutions

As you likely know, unfortunately not everyone has a supportive work environment, and feeling stuck in a miserable work situation can be an emotionally painful experience. Conditions at work may get so bad at times that you feel like quitting on the spot. This chaos can make it challenging to take the time to strategize and decide on the best way to handle workplace issues.

Making a plan to deal with toxic workplace behavior is crucial to your well-being, and considering your options may also help you feel less trapped. It's helpful for your plan to include things that are within your control—primarily modifications in the way you communicate and interact with your colleagues. This book includes practical tips you can start using today. The solutions provided are meant to decrease your levels of stress and frustration at work. At first, you may not feel comfortable using some of these techniques, but you may gain the confidence to try them out once you get into the habit of being assertive.

If you've gone through all channels of conflict resolution, yet your coworker's behavior continues to negatively affect you or the quality of your work, you may have to consider changing jobs. Even if it comes to this, you can take pride in the fact that you stood up for yourself and tried to resolve the issue. You can move on to a new workplace where your colleagues value your contributions and treat you with respect.

Evidence-Based

The suggestions in this book are rooted in evidence-based techniques, which means that research supports their effectiveness, according to the American Psychological Association. I've used several of these techniques while implementing cognitive behavioral therapy (CBT) to help people manage psychological problems in the workplace. More specifically, I've trained people in assertive communication and behavior to help them identify and set boundaries at work. Behavioral rehearsal helped the people I treated practice what they wanted to say and how they wanted to act in certain real-life situations.

Pioneers of CBT include psychologist Dr. Albert Ellis and psychiatrist Dr. Aaron T. Beck. They based their therapeutic techniques on the premise that an individual's thoughts about a situation influence their emotional and behavioral reactions. The Mayo Clinic notes that CBT focuses on transforming maladaptive, irrational thoughts into more balanced thoughts, so an individual's behavioral and emotional responses are more adaptive.

In a review paper explaining the benefits of assertiveness, Speed, Goldstein, and Goldfried reported that Dr. Joseph Wolpe, a psychiatrist and behavior therapy pioneer, advocated for assertiveness training to decrease anxiety. He developed an assessment to measure assertiveness with his colleague, psychologist Dr. Arnold Lazarus. According to the assessment, someone who can articulate their needs, say no, express how they feel, and show skill in conversation exhibits assertiveness. Psychologists Dr. Marvin Goldfried and Dr. Gerald Davison added a cognitive component to the understanding of assertiveness, suggesting that people might not be assertive due to fear of how speaking up could affect their relationships.

Speed, Goldstein, and Goldfried also cited research that shows that when people fail to act assertively, they have an increased chance of developing a psychological disorder. There is also a link between lack of assertiveness and poor self-esteem and relationships. Research supports assertiveness training as a method to improve these conditions, but even if a technique has been shown to be effective for some people, no approach is guaranteed to benefit all people.

When you use assertive behavior, especially when you may not have done so before, be prepared for how others may respond. Speed, Goldstein, and Goldfried point to research suggesting that gender can affect how assertive behavior is perceived, and that women who use assertive behavior in the workplace may be perceived negatively. Regardless of how people perceive you, increased assertiveness means that you can defend yourself, and the other person's response may say more about them than it does about you.

I've worked on both sides of the issues presented in this book. I've treated people who sought help because they realized their mental health issues were negatively impacting their workplace. I have also helped people who developed mental disorders due to the behavior of others in their work environment. The sections labeled "A Familiar Scene" are inspired by these experiences, but they are hypothetical and do not refer to any specific people or companies.

People living with the mental disorders discussed in this book often have poor boundaries and poor communication skills. That's why it's important to monitor your thoughts so that you're in a calm enough space to set boundaries and communicate clearly when you interact with them at work.

Actionable and Doable

The techniques in this book focus on communication and behavior during interpersonal interactions with your colleagues. You can put these practical tips into action immediately. Regardless of how your colleagues respond, knowing that you tried to make changes will likely empower you and give you the confidence to leave situations that are resistant to attempts at problem-solving.

Dialogue modeling focuses on assertive ways to express your needs. When someone treats you rudely, you may be surprised or wonder how to address issues calmly and effectively. Being assertive means expressing your thoughts, feelings, and preferences respectfully and without aggression. Being assertive can increase your self-esteem and decrease stress, anger, resentment, and other negative responses.

The Mayo Clinic provides helpful suggestions for how to use assertive language. The key is using "I" statements instead of placing blame on another person. Keep a calm tone, project confidence, and maintain good eye contact. Sometimes you may have to step away temporarily to think about how you want to respond. You may also practice what you plan to say until you get more comfortable.

The career development blog *Mind Tools* provides an approach to help you feel more comfortable using assertive communication. The first step is describing the problematic event or behavior. Next, state your feelings using "I" statements. Then, state your needs. Finally, describe the positive outcome for the person you're addressing if they meet your needs and the negative consequences if they don't. You may need to repeat yourself, in which case you can simply remind the person of the last conversation you had. The examples in the "Dialogue Model" sections include suggestions for assertive communication. You can use them as a model for situations that are specific to you.

At *PositivePsychology.com*, a blog that features articles written by mental health practitioners and researchers, Joaquín Selva describes various aspects of boundary setting. Setting boundaries involves establishing psychological or physical barriers with the intention to protect yourself from harm. Healthy boundaries can prevent or decrease burnout, anger, and resentment. Some people set boundaries that are too relaxed—answering intrusive questions, allowing people to speak to them in any manner, and letting people invade their personal space. Other people set boundaries that are too firm—acting mistrustful and isolating themselves from most people. They may not give people the chance to gain their trust. With loose boundaries at one end of the spectrum and rigid boundaries at the other, healthy boundaries usually fall right in the middle.

Boundaries are often influenced by your values, beliefs, and expectations for how you prefer to be treated. For example, if you respect people's personal space, but a colleague stands two inches from you, you may move further away or ask them to do so. If a team member speaks to you in a condescending tone, you may think it's disrespectful. You may value good working relationships and believe they improve productivity. When your colleague's behavior crosses this boundary, it may prompt you to address the issue immediately with assertive communication. These techniques are especially important when dealing with people with suspected personality disorders, as they often have poor boundaries.

Take a moment to think about your boundaries at work. With which colleagues have you established good boundaries? With whom do you need to set boundaries?

Quiz: Let's Review

Do you think productivity issues in your workplace are influenced by the toxic behaviors of some of your coworkers? Take this quiz to assess your work situation:

1. Do your colleagues routinely steal your ideas, talk over you, or treat you in other rude ways?

2. Are roles poorly defined, leaving you to take on multiple duties?

3. Do you frequently receive blame but rarely receive praise or support?

4. Are you asked to meet unrealistic standards with little or no concern for your well-being?

5. Are you afraid to speak up and voice your concerns?

6. Do you get sad, anxious, or angry or have physical symptoms like headaches and stomachaches when you think about work?

7. Do you witness your colleagues quitting shortly after being hired?

The more questions you've agreed with, the higher the indication is that you work in a toxic environment where productivity is stifled. Consider trying out the suggestions in this book to help you resolve issues directly with colleagues when you can. You may have to address some issues with your manager or others at a higher level of authority.

If none of these efforts resolve your problems, consider developing an exit plan. For example, you may search for other jobs and build up your savings. If you need professional guidance to deal with the psychological toll of workplace issues, seek the help of a licensed mental health professional.

Chapter 2

Needs Constant Reassurance

Does one of your colleagues usually expect the worst? Do they ask constant questions that make you doubt your abilities? Do they hold up the team's progress because they're afraid to approach a manager for approval on a necessary step in a project? When someone checks up on you frequently, delays important work, or has such a negative outlook for themselves and the team, you're bound to get frustrated.

A colleague who needs constant reassurance may have an anxiety disorder. Being aware of the symptoms of a possible anxiety disorder may give you some insight into your coworker's behavior. Because of their own fears or insecurity about getting a job done, they will often ask you to reassure them that everything is on track and that things will turn out well in the end. The behavior of a coworker with a possible anxiety disorder is often driven by perfectionism, self-doubt, and an exaggerated fear of losing control.

In this chapter, you will learn specific techniques to improve your communication with someone with a possible anxiety disorder and how to set boundaries when interacting with them. You'll come away with some techniques to separate your work life from your personal life. You'll also learn how to prevent your colleague's insecurity from diminishing your confidence about your own competence.

A Familiar Scene

John manages a team of research analysts at a market research firm. Over the past few months, several analysts have asked about incorporating new research approaches into their data analysis for better accuracy and efficiency. John tells them each time that he's worried that the research director won't approve of these new methods. He fears that training will be too expensive and new research methods will take too long to learn. This is not the first time John has expressed fear of approaching the research director on behalf of his team.

John often speaks with a sense of urgency, and at times his tone comes across as condescending when he speaks to his team. During meetings, he often speaks so fast that team members have trouble keeping up, and he appears flustered when people ask questions he didn't expect. John seems so overwhelmed at times that he has trouble remembering what he said even moments earlier. Sometimes he can be seen literally running from office to office, as if an emergency has occurred. Other times, he hides in his office when he's frustrated or nervous.

The analyst team is currently working on a new project for a food and beverage company. John asks the analysts to provide him with updates on their progress several times each day, even though there are no indications the project is behind schedule. He interrupts analysts eating lunch at their desks with questions and updates about various work issues. He even e-mails and calls some analysts at home after work hours.

Even when the analysts have double-checked their research analyses and found consistent results, John insists that they run the analyses a third time. He constantly asks, "What if . . . ?" and seems to anticipate the worst-case scenario each time. He also advises them to back up all of their data and doc-umentation on multiple drives, which they already do. He frequently tells the story of how he lost an account because of a mishap with the data his team collected. This error occurred at a different company, long before he started managing this team. After his analysts assure him that they appreciate his advice and are following it to prevent such a mistake, John continues to ask them if they're following through on his instructions.

John's anxiety has spread throughout the team, and they are starting to ask each other the same questions John asks. Some analysts have become mistrustful of others and doubt their own ability. Since they are afraid to express their feelings to John, team members start to take their issues out on each other. Some team members have started to call out sick, and others work overtime and delay their vacations to try to meet the deadline.

John tells his analysts not to move forward with anything else until he runs the analyses himself. When John gets the same results as his analysts, he tells them to start on the presentation. Due to John repeating the processes and duplicating their work, the team must now make up for lost time as the deadline quickly approaches. This feeds John's anxiety even more, and he starts to push them all harder. John can't understand why his team has fallen behind when he believes he made such an effort to keep everything on track.

Solving the Problem

Working with a colleague who has a possible anxiety disorder can be frustrating and stressful. The way they interact with you may lead you to doubt your ability. Their frequent check-ins and questions may make you feel as if they don't trust you to do a good job. You also probably have less time to focus on your work because so much time is spent engaging with and reassuring your colleague.

It will be helpful to know how to agree on project expectations and set realistic goals when working with this colleague. You might also consider ways to balance the demands of work life with responsibilities in your personal life. For example, determine how often you will provide updates and when you will be available to them by e-mail and phone.

It's important to remember that the behavior of a coworker struggling with a possible anxiety disorder is often driven by their own fear. They can change their behavior, but they must make the decision to do so. You can't control how your coworker behaves, but you can decide not to let their behavior change the way you think about yourself and your ability to get work done.

Dialogue Model

The following examples focus on different ways to use assertive communication with your colleague. You'll learn how to point out their problematic behavior, express how you feel about it, state the alternative that you prefer, and articulate why it's good for you and your colleague to make some changes.

A manager with a possible anxiety disorder will have a similar style of interacting with mostly everyone in your workplace. They typically ask for frequent updates to soothe their fears about the process and outcome of each project. They may also have unrealistic expectations of themselves and others, hesitate to delegate duties, ask you to make unnecessary revisions, and insist that you do things exactly the way they would do them. These behaviors can lead to delays, missed deadlines, and lower team morale. These results may make you begin to doubt your own ability and that of your coworkers.

Manager: The last time we spoke, you told me you were getting ready to analyze the data. I need you to e-mail me with your progress on this task every hour so that I know we're on schedule to meet the deadline.

You: I understand your concern about meeting the deadline, and I want us to meet it, too. But when you ask me to e-mail you every hour, I feel overwhelmed because it's hard to stay on track with my analysis when I have to stop to check in with you. I'd prefer that we speak about the project in person at the end of each day.

Manager: I just want to make sure that we'll meet the deadline and that our analyses are accurate. What if the analyses don't provide the client with any insight? If we don't deliver accurate results, we'll never win another account from that company.

You: I want us to turn in a great project, too. If we touch base in person at the end of the day instead of e-mailing each hour, I'll have more time to focus on making sure the analyses are accurate. That way, the client will be happy and we'll earn their business again.

In this scenario, the employee leads the conversation by expressing empathy for the manager's priorities and concerns and assures the manager that they have the same goal—they both want to meet the deadline. Once that is clarified, the employee expresses how they feel and offers an alternative way to update the manager on their progress.

Much like a manager, a peer or support staff with a possible anxiety disorder will often try to anticipate problems so they can solve them. As their anxiety builds, however, they might ask questions that make other people feel uncomfortable or put on the spot. They are full of "what ifs." Even though they don't manage you, the behavior of a peer or support staff with a possible anxiety disorder can still feel intense because of how much time you spend with them. When this happens, anxiety could spread to you and other members of your team.

Peer: Are you sure the data has been coded correctly? Let me look at it before I move on to the analysis.

You: *This is the second time you've asked me today. I thought we cleared this up the first time you asked me.*

Peer: *I just hate making mistakes. What if I have to redo the analysis? I'd hate to do that because of incorrect codes that we could have fixed before I started.*

You: *When you ask me the same question after I've already assured you I'm doing my best, I feel concerned that my ability to do this job is in doubt. I'd prefer that you recheck the codes after I finish coding everything. That way, I can focus on accuracy during the first round of coding. When you recheck the data during the second round, it'll add an extra layer of accuracy to the work I've already done.*

The employee leads the conversation in the previous scenario by identifying the problematic behavior in objective terms and stating that they've been asked about the data twice on the same day. When the peer continues to assume the worst and ask the same question repeatedly, the employee expresses their feelings, states their preferences, and points out how an alternative method of checking in will be helpful for both of them and for the success of the project.

Support staff: Your client called. She said she wanted to speak with you directly.

You: Did she say what it was about?

Support staff: No. But what if they're not happy with the timeline? What if they want to take their account to another research firm?

You: When you ask questions like that, I feel overwhelmed. Going forward, I'd prefer that you report to me exactly what a client says and if they have a specific concern. Then we can both use our energy to focus on the most important things that need immediate attention.

In the previous scenario, the support staff bombards the employee with what they think may go wrong with the project, based on limited information. Their colleague expresses their feelings, states their preferences, and then points out why this alternative approach will be more helpful for both of them.

Setting Boundaries

A large part of setting boundaries with a colleague who may have an anxiety disorder involves separating their insecurity from your own. Another component involves separating your work life from your personal life.

♦ **Discuss expectations.** Before you begin a project, discuss expectations and concerns that you and your coworker have. This gives you both a chance to agree on what is expected from each of you in your work on the project and to acknowledge potential obstacles to success. Although you can't prepare for everything that could happen along the way, setting and discussing clear expectations can help you to better meet goals.

♦ **Anticipate concerns.** Make it clear to your coworker that you intend to do an outstanding job and determine ways to address any concerns that arise. This may help soothe your coworker's fears, as they tend to focus on the worst-case scenario. This is also an opportunity to address any unrealistic expectations they may have before you find yourself putting the effort into meeting them. Give a rationale for why your colleague's expectation is unrealistic, and focus on the available resources and the time that would be lost trying to meet it. Highlight how creating more realistic expectations would be more efficient.

- **Develop a quality assurance measure.** A checklist for a manager is an example of a quality assurance measure. This can possibly ease your manager's concern about project outcomes and ensure that their assessment of your performance is based on an objective measure. If your manager is not happy with the job you completed or needs you to make changes, they can provide specific, constructive feedback based on the quality assurance measure.

- **Create a timeline.** Agree to touch base with each other at designated times according to the timeline. This can keep both of you on track while preventing unnecessary interruptions.

- **Ask for help.** If you run into a problem you can't solve on your own, let your coworker know as soon as possible so you can start figuring out a solution. You may be inclined to hide any issues from your coworker, but this can make the situation worse.

- **Eat lunch outside the office.** Coworkers may ask you work-related questions if you eat lunch at your desk. Going out for lunch signals that you are dedicated to self-care and taking the break you need before continuing with your workday.

- **Know your department's policies.** If there are no departmental guidelines to follow, decide the conditions (e.g., emergencies) under which you will answer after-hours communication from colleagues. This may be a personal decision that you choose not to share with your coworkers.

- **Set your voicemail and e-mail greetings.** Sometimes you may choose to let your colleague know how you respond to workplace correspondence. Consider indicating on your voicemail how soon you will return calls. You may also set automated e-mail replies after hours indicating when you will be available to check e-mail. For example, your automated response may read, "This e-mail is not checked on weekends or between the hours of 5:00 p.m. and 9:00 a.m. on weekdays."

If You Remember One Thing . . .

When working with someone who may have an anxiety disorder, remember that their behavior is often motivated by self-doubt and a fear of losing control. This may help you separate your coworker's insecurities from your own, focus on your work, and think clearly enough to handle obstacles if they do occur.

Chapter 3

Can't Focus on Tasks

Are you working with someone who seems distracted, forgetful, and unmotivated? Do they seem to fall further behind, leaving more for you to do? If so, you may be tired of covering for them or waiting for them to complete their work.

Difficulty concentrating can be a symptom of several mental disorders. Someone who finds it difficult to focus on tasks in the workplace could be struggling with major depressive disorder, bipolar disorder, an anxiety disorder, or ADHD. Remember that a qualified mental health professional is the only one who can diagnose someone with a mental disorder. However, learning about the symptoms your colleagues are experiencing may help you understand their behavior. You may not take their behavior as personally as you would if you didn't have this insight. Instead of getting upset, you can focus on getting your work done.

In this chapter you'll learn ways to identify colleagues who can't focus on tasks, especially those who may have major depressive disorder or bipolar disorder. The behavior of someone who can't focus on tasks because of a mood disorder is often influenced by impaired memory—difficulty retaining or recalling information. When depressed, your colleague may also be distracted by negative thoughts about themselves, others, and their environment. If they experience mania or hypomania, their thoughts may seem to race. You will also learn how to improve your communication and set boundaries when interacting with colleagues who are displaying these symptoms. This information can help you intervene as quickly as possible, before productivity in the workplace worsens.

A Familiar Scene

Kyra is a medical billing specialist in a hospital. Over the past few years, she has built a reputation for being a hard worker who processes claims quickly and efficiently.

For the past three weeks, Kyra has come in late. At first, she was 15 minutes late, but by the third week, she is coming in 30 minutes late most days of the week. When she arrives, she appears groggy and it takes her a while to settle in. When she tries to pick up from where she left off, she often has difficulty finding what she needs to complete the task. Her workspace is cluttered and covered with various reminders and piles of paperwork.

Kyra takes frequent breaks and tells her colleagues she needs to clear her head. When colleagues ask her to join them for lunch, she usually declines and chooses to eat by herself. Some coworkers have walked in on her napping in the employee lounge when she's not on designated break time. However, these breaks don't seem to help her gain focus. Kyra has asked several colleagues to remind her of basic computer functions she used to have no problem completing. She now sometimes forgets how to use the computer program that generates the claims.

When Kyra's colleagues walk past her workspace, she appears to be staring blankly at her computer screen. At team meetings, she appears not to pay attention. When the manager asks Kyra what she thinks about ideas for improved patient care, she asks the manager to repeat the question and looks confused. This also happens when her colleagues ask her to share an opinion.

When patients call with questions about their bill, Kyra loses track of what they're talking about. Taking notes isn't always helpful—she often can't remember what she's just heard—and most of her notes appear jumbled and are hard to read. Kyra often puts patients on hold while she tries to find an answer for them. Sometimes she forgets they're on hold, and other times she gets so frustrated she transfers the patients to her colleagues.

Kyra becomes most stressed when she works on multiple projects. She has started to stay late at work to finish projects that should have been completed days prior. Yet, she just makes more mistakes, frequently entering the wrong code for medical services received by a patient.

Patients have complained to Kyra's manager that they were billed for the wrong services. Some insurance companies have rejected a few of her claims. Under further review, Kyra's manager discovers that she made several careless mistakes and that she mixed up medical codes on several bills. The manager is concerned that the hospital's stellar reputation is at risk due to Kyra's mistakes.

Kyra's colleagues are also getting frustrated with her because they don't understand the changes in her behavior and why she puts them in risky and awkward positions. She has sometimes asked them not to tell their manager about her naps and lateness. She has also asked them to file some of her claims so that she can catch up. At first, most of her colleagues didn't mind and wanted to help. Now they don't feel comfortable lying to their manager or taking on work that isn't their own.

Kyra desperately wants to catch up on her work and become productive again, but she just can't seem to focus.

Solving the Problem

Working with a colleague who has difficulty focusing can be tough. At first, you may try to help your colleague. You may give them reminders or agree not to expose their mistakes. If the problem continues, you may become resentful that your colleague's behavior is delaying your own progress.

It's best to catch the issue as soon as possible. Identifying a problem with someone who can't focus may be easier if the employee has a history of performing efficiently. But that doesn't always happen, since it can take some time before a noticeable pattern develops. If your colleague's concentration problems are brief and only occasional, it may not be cause for concern. However, once a pattern occurs that affects productivity in the workplace, it's time to address the issue.

Be sure to speak with your colleague privately, avoiding calling attention to the issue in front of other staff members. Also try not to come across as condescending. It's helpful to consider the impact of the workspace, workload, and methods of communication when addressing this issue. Your colleague may get distracted if they are located near a noisy part of the office. They may also be overwhelmed by your unrealistic expectations. It's also possible that offering multiple methods of communication may help your colleague stay on track, since their memory is likely impaired. They may find it difficult to remember what you say but find it easier to refer to your e-mail.

Dialogue Model

In the following models, you'll learn how to use assertive statements to show empathy for your colleague, while addressing issues related to delays in the workflow. You'll also learn how to motivate colleagues when they are the first point of contact on a project. Notice the assertive use of "I" statements, expression of preferences versus demands, and reasoning for stating the preferences.

When managers have difficulty focusing on tasks, they can cause work to get backlogged. This is especially the case if part of their job is to review your work before it's considered complete. Managers can become defensive when they don't want to be perceived as less competent than the employees they're supervising. Sometimes managers may not bring attention to their issues and avoid acknowledging their part in the problem. It's important to make sure you're not held accountable for their delays. Ideally, your manager acknowledges their behavior. A responsible manager neither holds you responsible for their issues nor pressures you into delaying your own work to cover for them.

Manager: There's so much to get done this time of the year. Don't expect me to sign off on your work right away. I'll get to it when I can.

You: I understand it's busy this time of year, but I can only file claims once you sign off on my work.

Manager: I'll review your work as soon as I can. There's no rush for you to get through the claims. You can spread them out. Why don't you work on the quality assurance project we started last month?

You: I don't want to overwhelm you. I appreciate you telling me that it may take you longer than usual to review my files. It is busy, but I prefer to start on claims as they come in, even if they won't be filed until you review them. I want to make sure you won't hold it against me if I turn in the claims sooner than you'd like.

In the previous scenario, the manager needs to review their colleague's work before it's considered complete. The manager is having trouble completing work on time and tries to get their colleague to match their pace. The colleague emphasizes that they understand their manager's situation but expresses their preference to continue to submit the claims as they come in. The colleague then confirms that they won't be penalized for submitting them that way.

A peer who can't focus on tasks might hold up the workflow. If you're part of a team, you may not be able to proceed until your peer adds their contribution to the project. You can show empathy for them in a conversation about the project, while also expressing your needs.

> *Peer: I just can't seem to catch up on these claims and work on the quality assurance project at the same time. Once I get through one batch of claims, another batch needs to be processed. Then there's never time to work on the project.*

> *You: It's really busy this time of year, but our project presentation is coming up soon.*

> *Peer: I just don't know what to do. I'm so far behind and I'm tired all the time.*

> *You: I can imagine it must be hard for you to focus on the project and catch up on your claims, especially since it's so busy and you said you're tired all the time. But I feel overwhelmed. I'd prefer to get the summary of the patient satisfaction surveys from you as soon as possible so we can finish the presentation on time. Maybe you can speak to the manager and see if there's something she can do to help.*

In the previous scenario, a colleague's peer confides in them that they are having difficulty focusing on multiple tasks. The colleague expresses empathy but still points out that their project is due soon. They state their feelings and preferences and offer their peer a suggestion on how to get help.

A support staff member may cause project delays if they are the first point of contact for your customers or clients. They may fail to pass on messages, and you may not be informed with the most current information you need to do your work. You may also have to work harder to make a good impression if the support staff gave consumers a poor first impression of your company's brand. Express empathy, but also state what you need to get your job done.

> *Support staff:* My phone never stops ringing! Sometimes I can't even remember who called. I try writing it down, but then I forget to pass the messages on.

> *You:* I understand how busy it can get. But for me to file the claims correctly, it's important to know as soon as possible if patients have any concerns or questions about their bills.

> *Support staff:* Well, everyone is just going to have to wait. I'm the only receptionist here.

> *You:* I understand it gets busy at times. But I'd prefer to know right away if someone has a question about the claims I've filed so that I can help them resolve their issues as soon as possible. Otherwise, we may get more calls and even complaints from frustrated patients wondering why

they haven't received a call back. Maybe you can speak to your supervisor and share your concerns about how being the only receptionist here makes it difficult to manage so many calls.

In the previous situation, a support staff member is overwhelmed with being the only receptionist in a busy office. Their colleague expresses empathy and explains why they need to receive their messages as soon as possible. When the receptionist gets more frustrated, their colleague reiterates why the messages need to be delivered in a timely manner and speaks about the negative consequences if messages are delayed. The colleague then offers a suggestion for how the receptionist could voice their concerns.

Setting Boundaries

Setting boundaries with someone who can't focus on tasks involves identifying which duties are your responsibility and which are your colleague's. For example, when a colleague falls behind schedule due to their inability to focus, it may be tempting to do some of their work if it means moving things along, or you may be tempted to keep pace with them to avoid conflict.

Another aspect of setting boundaries is asking for what you need to get your job done. This is especially the case if your colleague causes delays when you need their input before you can complete your own task. For example, you may need to edit your work to include your colleague's suggestions.

A third component of setting boundaries involves fixing environmental issues that may impact your colleague's ability to focus.

◆ **Follow up conversations in writing.** After you speak to your colleague about what you need them to do for a project, follow up with an e-mail. Be sure to use a tone that comes across as helpful, not condescending. This technique gives your colleague another way of processing information they may have missed. This also provides your colleague with a chance to ask questions that may not have occurred to them the first time they received your instructions. Your colleague may also feel more comfortable asking some questions via e-mail rather than speaking to you in person.

◆ **Learn how often to give reminders.** You may be tempted to frequently remind your colleague about due dates, but try not to be overbearing. If your reminders don't work the first time, you may fall into a cycle of getting more frustrated with each subsequent reminder you give. This can increase your levels of stress.

- **Set limits.** Decide how many times you can afford to give your colleague a break. You may want to give them a chance to make up for their lack of attention on a project, but don't let this become the standard. Define a reasonable limit; after it is reached, have a plan to discuss the issue with your colleague and start to develop solutions.

- **Document delays in writing.** If your colleague speaks to you about a delay on their end, be sure to follow up in an e-mail. If your work is affected by their delay and you are blamed for it, the e-mail may help demonstrate where the delay originated.

- **Consider changes to the environment.** This may make it easier for your coworker to concentrate. For example, your colleague may find it almost impossible to work in a noisy environment. Consider moving your colleague's workspace to a quieter area if possible.

- **Assess your colleague's workload.** Think about whether or not your expectations are realistic. Consider reducing their workload if possible.

- **Offer some flexibility.** Some people's ability to concentrate is worse in the mornings; for others, it's worse in the afternoon. Find out when your colleague works the best and encourage them to complete activities that require attention to detail during those times.

♦ **Separate your duties.** Make sure you're not taking on tasks to pick up the slack for your colleague. Having empathy for them doesn't mean you have to do their share of the work.

If You Remember One Thing . . .

Try to remember that someone with difficulty focusing on tasks is typically not doing it out of spite. Their memory may be compromised, making it difficult to retain information. Provide multiple methods of communication, consider changes to the workplace setting and workload, and avoid taking on work that isn't yours. Still, there's only so much you can do until your colleague addresses the root cause of their issues.

Chapter 4

Struggles with Follow-Through

Is there a colleague who seems scattered and inconsistent in the way they manage their time at work? They may always seem to be on the go yet never seem to make much progress. If that's the case, you may be fed up with your coworker's backlogged work and frequent requests for extensions.

Difficulty with time-management can be a symptom of several mental disorders. A colleague who finds it difficult to follow through on tasks may be struggling with ADHD, major depressive disorder, bipolar disorder, or an anxiety disorder. A qualified mental health professional is the only one who can diagnose someone with a mental disorder resulting in issues with time-management. However, learning about possible reasons for this behavior may better prepare you for interacting with your coworker. Rather than suffering the consequences of your colleague's delays, you can come up with ways to work around their behavior.

In this chapter you'll learn how to combat problems associated with a colleague who has difficulty completing tasks, with an emphasis on someone who may have ADHD. Someone who has time-management issues due to ADHD usually processes information differently from someone who doesn't have the disorder. These differences usually occur because their neural networks did not develop in the typical manner during childhood.

Strengthening communication and boundaries with your colleague involves separating your responsibilities from those of your colleague, minimizing interruptions, creating timelines, examining barriers in the work environment, and planning for alternative ways to get work done.

A Familiar Scene

Michael is a production assistant for a production company working on an upcoming film. His responsibilities change from day to day; he can be responsible for answering phones, reading scripts, preparing the set, making reservations, running errands, and other administrative tasks.

Michael has problems with being on time consistently. On Monday and Tuesday, he is on time, but on Wednesday, he comes in 30 minutes late and is already behind schedule. The producer asks Michael to make 20 copies of the most recent version of the script and to have them ready to distribute to staff by 1:00 p.m. The producer specifies that each 120-page script also needs to be bound. Michael is also tasked with scheduling interviews for an open intern position. The producer asks Michael if he wants one of the current interns to help with the copies. Michael declines the offer of help and states that he can get the job done himself.

After Michael settles in, he starts calling back interview candidates and figures he can make the copies later. He underestimates the amount of time it will take for him to copy and bind the scripts. After scheduling several interviews with potential interns, Michael decides to step out to pick up some lunch since the restaurant is right across the street. By the time he starts on the copies, it's 12:30 p.m.

Figuring he doesn't have enough time to finish the copies, Michael stops after four copies and goes back to scheduling interviews. The producer on the film— also Michael's supervisor— discovers that Michael did not add some of the interview appointments into the producer's schedule. Michael can't finish the copies, so the producer asks an intern to finish them. The cast and crew are supposed to do a table read of the script, but they reschedule since the scripts aren't ready by 1:00 p.m.

On Thursday, the producer asks Michael to make sure all appointments for the intern interview are scheduled and put on his calendar. Later that day, Michael receives two calls from people stating they had been contacted for an interview but never received a call back confirming their interview time.

One of the callers becomes skeptical because of the lack of organization.

On Friday, the producer asks Michael to write coverage for three scripts by the following Monday. Michael reads two scripts but can't finish the third. He writes coverage for one of the scripts but is not able to finish coverage for the other script he read. Michael asks the producer for an extension. Instead of giving Michael the extension, he asks the intern to finish the coverage.

As filming progresses, the producer is concerned that if Michael is trusted to take on more tasks, he may set the schedule back. Other colleagues are frustrated with Michael because the producer asks them to complete his tasks.

When Michael agrees to a task, he believes he can finish it on time. He doesn't want to delay the film in any way, but he just can't seem to follow through on tasks.

Solving the Problem

The behavior of a manager, peer, or support staff with poor time-management skills can cause extra work for you as you make up for what they didn't finish. Their lack of follow-through may also mean you get started on your work later than planned. Your colleague may also project their shame onto those they manage and blame others for their problems at work. Still, it's important to remember that people with time-management problems due to ADHD often want to deliver their projects on time but find it difficult because of the way their brains process information.

Ideally, avoid taking responsibility for your coworker's delay. If a delay occurs, sometimes your colleague may acknowledge their role in it. You and your coworker can acknowledge how this will affect the workflow and how you can move forward. Change may be more difficult with a manager with poor time-management skills. They may be reluctant to acknowledge the impact of their behavior on the workflow. In this situation, it can be helpful to negotiate in order to reach a solution that benefits both of you.

Dialogue Model

In the following models, you'll learn how to make suggestions that offer a positive resolution for you and your colleague. You'll also learn how to avoid taking on extra work. Lastly, you'll get some tips on how to make sure your colleague understands how you're expecting them to carry out an assignment. Notice the use of assertive communication techniques.

A manager who has difficulty with time-management may get distracted or delayed and tell you about an assignment, expecting you to complete it on short notice. If you ask for more time, they may try to blame you or find fault with the way you do your job, possibly due to their own hurt and shame about not being able to meet goals. In this situation, try to reach a compromise that doesn't put you behind schedule based on their lack of follow-through. Follow up the conversation with an e-mail to document where the delay started. The e-mail should summarize what you discussed in person, and the tone should read as if you're follow-ing up to make sure both parties have agreed to what was discussed. You may start with, "Per our conver-sation . . ." or "To follow up on our conversation . . .".

> *Manager: I have another script for you. The pro-ducer needs coverage for this one and the others by tomorrow morning. You can handle that, right?*

> *You: I've already been assigned five scripts to read and the coverage for all of them is also due tomor-row, as you know. I still have two more scripts to get through.*

> *Manager: I've been meaning to get this one to you since last week, but things just got so busy. The producer still needs the coverage by tomorrow, so what's one more? By now, it should only take you a few hours to read it and write coverage.*

> *You: I understand that sometimes it can get so busy that you may forget to share tasks with me. But if you need me to write coverage for a script, I'd prefer you tell me as soon as possible next time*

so that I have enough time to turn in good work. Maybe you could ask the producer to push back the due date for one of the two scripts I have left. This way, I can still turn in the quality of coverage our producer likes.

The manager gives their colleague a last-minute script in the previous scenario. Even though the manager forgot to give the script to their colleague the week before, they don't change the due date to compensate for the additional work and their lack of follow-through. The colleague empathizes with their manager and states their preferences for next time to prevent this from happening again. The colleague then negotiates for more time by highlighting how this resolution will help them deliver the results the producer wants.

A peer who has difficulty with time-management may ask you for help completing their work. They may be forgetful and ask you questions to help guide them through the process. You may want to help them, but their questions may interrupt your workflow, leaving you with less time to complete your own work.

Peer: Last week we got so many scripts to read that sometimes it's hard for me to remember what I've just read. How do you keep up with it all when it's time for you to write coverage?

You: Most of the time I make notes as I read, and other times the story is so interesting I just remember everything.

Peer: When we had our training, what did the development director say about writing notes on the structure and pacing? I should have written it down and now I can't remember.

You: When you ask questions while I'm in the middle of reading, I feel worried I'm not going to have enough time to get through this big pile of scripts. I prefer to focus my energy on getting through as much of the work as I can. Maybe it would help you to follow the templates in the manual they gave us.

In the previous scenario, a colleague is interrupted by a peer who asks several questions about how to do their work. The colleague states their preferences to get their own work done and suggests their peer consult the manual.

A support staff member may have difficulty remembering details of an assignment. Ask them to repeat back to you their understanding of the task at hand. Try not to come across as condescending. This way, you can assess how well they understand your instructions and offer clarification if needed. If they fail to follow through, it is more difficult for them to blame you for not giving clear instructions.

Support staff: *Okay. I know you have a table read this afternoon, so I'll start on the scripts right away.*

You: *Just so I can make sure we're on the same page, what is your understanding of the assignment?*

Support staff: *You said you need 25 copies of the updated scripts and that you want them bound.*

You: *Yes, and I also asked that you hand them out to everyone by 2:00 p.m. today, in time for the table read. Please let me know if you have any questions. Thanks.*

In the previous scenario, the colleague makes sure the support staff understands what is requested of them. The tone comes across as helpful, not condescending.

Setting Boundaries

Setting boundaries with someone who has poor time-management skills involves separating your responsibilities from theirs, minimizing interruptions, creating timelines, and devising alternative ways to get work done. This often involves being knowledge-able about the workflow.

Another part of setting boundaries involves examining your colleague's work environment to identify and remove barriers to productivity. This is especially important if you're in a management position.

♦ **Be knowledgeable about the workflow.** Know each colleague's role in the workflow, especially if you are a manager. Know what tasks must be completed at each step in the process and who is responsible for completing them. Acknowledge that some colleagues' work may be delayed if another coworker can't complete their part on time.

♦ **Create timelines.** Specify the date and time that you need a task to be completed. Set the due date for a bit before you actually need it all done, to give you a cushion for addressing any issues that might occur. Break down complicated tasks into different phases, which can help your colleague stay on track. They can adjust their progress depending on where they are on the timeline.

♦ **Document changes in the timeline by e-mail.** Note changes that are due to a delay, and note any of your attempts at reminding your colleague of the work that is due. This is particularly helpful if you are at risk of being blamed for not managing the problem.

- **Be easy to confide in.** If you manage others, let your colleagues know they can feel comfortable confiding in you if they have difficulty completing a task. Let them know that you will try to help. When your colleagues don't fear your reaction, they are more likely to ask for help when obstacles prevent them from getting their work done.

- **Check progress at meetings.** For team projects, consider holding meetings where everyone provides an update on where they are in the project. These check-ins highlight their accountability to the team and allow them to showcase their expertise. This meeting could also be used to generate solutions for colleagues that feel stuck in their work.

- **Strike a balance between coaching and micromanaging.** When someone fails to complete a task, it may become more difficult for you to trust that they will do a better job the next time. You may be tempted to check in on them more often. However, your colleague may also experience low motivation if they sense you're monitoring their every move.

◆ **Set limits.** The first time your colleague fails to complete a task, you may be somewhat under-standing. But resentment can build and work can continue to pile up if a pattern of behavior sets in. Determine your limit for how long you will accept your colleague's behavior. When that boundary is crossed, be ready to address and resolve the issue with them.

◆ **Discuss the consequences.** Let your colleague know how their lack of follow-through affects the workflow and other staff members. Let them know what is at risk if they fail to follow through a second time. Speak about the consequences of not being consistent in completing tasks on time.

◆ **Identify and remove barriers.** Ask your colleague to identify what got in the way of their comple-tion of the task. Help them come up with ways to overcome those barriers. Ask your colleague to identify how they will work differently the next time.

If You Remember One Thing . . .

Create a timeline for task completion and acknowledge how your coworker's lack of follow-through will affect the workflow. Identify whose work will be delayed if one colleague falls behind schedule. This way you can address the issue as soon as possible and devise a plan to get back on track.

Chapter 5

Says One Thing but Does Another

Do you work with someone who can't seem to keep their promises? Maybe they told you they would hand in their report on time, yet they leave you scrambling to meet a deadline when they can't deliver. Perhaps they promised you would never have to do certain tasks but ask you to do them anyway. You're probably tired of their excuses and cleaning up the messes they make. It's even more frustrating when your colleague seems to get away with this behavior. This happens because they are often charming and twist situations to benefit themselves.

A coworker like this who exhibits passive-aggressive behavior may have a personality disorder, such as borderline personality disorder (BPD) or narcissistic personality disorder (NPD). It's a mental health professional's job to diagnose these mental disorders, but learning how to recognize when a colleague may have a personality disorder can help you stay calm under pressure. You can respond to your colleague's behavior from a place of strength, rather than a place of anger or another negative feeling.

In this chapter, you'll learn how to identify a coworker who may have a personality disorder, and you'll find ways to deal with their often passive-aggressive behavior. Strengthening communication and boundaries with this colleague involves keeping personal information to yourself, refusing to let them feed off your emotions, and avoiding getting caught in the middle of conflict.

A Familiar Scene

Caroline is a manager at a clothing store. Over the past few weeks, four employees have quit. Caroline's staff have had to take on extra work while she scrambles to hire new workers. After several weeks, she fills all four open positions, and Marlena is one of the new staff members.

Caroline takes an immediate liking to Marlena and gives her a warm welcome. Some of the staff start to notice that Caroline gives Marlena the best schedules and least stressful duties. Caroline often tells Marlena personal things, even though it seems to make Marlena uncomfortable. She goes into detail about the arguments she has with her boyfriend and says nasty things about some of their colleagues. She's very intrusive and asks Marlena many personal questions; she wants to know about Marlena's family background, if she is dating, and why she took the job. Although Marlena is unsure of how to respond, she thinks it's harmless to share a few personal things about herself. Caroline finds out that Marlena is a college student and is working at the store to help pay her tuition. She tells Marlena how much she admires her ambition and assures her that she won't have any problems requesting time off to study.

One week, Caroline receives a request for time off from Marlena. The request is made three weeks in advance, and Marlena tells Caroline she needs to take off three days to study for final exams. Caroline doesn't approve the request until one day before Marlena requested to take off. Instead of considering the generous notice Marlena gave, Caroline takes it personally. She becomes angry at Marlena, believing she is inconsiderate for putting her needs before the needs of the store. However, she doesn't directly express her anger.

While Marlena is away, Caroline tells Marlena's colleagues that she took off with short notice, and because of her, they have to do extra work. Caroline fails to use the three weeks' advance notice to adjust the schedules. When Marlena returns to work, she is surprised that her colleagues are acting strangely toward her. They seem angry at her and tell her about the extra work they had to do in her absence. When Marlena tells them that she gave three weeks' advance notice, her coworkers say that Caroline never told them this.

Upon Marlena's return, Caroline acts cold toward her and Marlena can't understand why. Caroline refuses to return Marlena's greetings, rarely makes eye contact when she speaks to Marlena, and glares when she does look at her. She decides to place Marlena in the cashier position—after promising she would never do this—knowing that this position makes her anxious and likely to perform poorly. Marlena makes several mistakes at the register, and Caroline criticizes her but refuses to change her schedule. Marlena depends on the job for a portion of her tuition but just can't take the stress anymore. She finally puts in her two-week notice. Marlena suspects Caroline won't give her a good reference, so she has a friend call Caroline and pretend to ask for one. Sure enough, Caroline only has negative things to say about Marlena. Marlena decides not to use her as a reference in the future and chooses another manager to give her a reference.

Caroline has a hard time accepting that Marlena will be the fifth staff person to quit in the past three months and doesn't appear to understand why she left.

Solving the Problem

One of the most challenging things about dealing with a colleague who engages in passive-aggressive behavior is that their hostility may not be obvious to others. You could end up being seen as the aggressor when you try to speak up for yourself. Since this colleague feeds off your reactions, finding a way not to overreact to their behavior is crucial. It's good to find a way to document your conversations with them in writing, as people who behave in a passive-aggressive manner are often known for telling you one thing and doing another.

You're probably used to this colleague getting into your personal business. People with personality disorders that consist of passive-aggressive behavior often push the limits of others by disrespecting their boundaries. They will keep pushing to see how much you'll take, so the sooner you address issues with them, the better.

If your colleague has a personality disorder, their behavior can be highly resistant to change. This is usually because they've held on to these behaviors for a long time and are unlikely to acknowledge their role in dysfunctional workplaces. You may have to avoid a colleague like this and only spend a short amount of time interacting when it's impossible to avoid them.

Dialogue Model

In the following examples, you'll learn how to remind colleagues of agreements they made, avoid being pitted against another colleague, and keep your personal business private.

A manager with possible borderline personality disorder (BPD) or narcissistic personality disorder (NPD) will typically disregard what they previously promised you. Because people with these disorders have often suffered childhood trauma and betrayal, their perception of trust and what it means to keep their word is twisted. They often break their promises when you are most vulnerable, and their behavior can even sabotage your career. It's best to secure any promises from them in writing, remind them of any agreements you made with them, and then provide the written documentation if they try to change up on you. If you need to escalate the situation to your colleague's supervisor, you will then have some evidence to support your claim.

> **Manager:** *I need you to help out on the registers. This sale is bringing everybody in all day. Look at that! I really need you to pitch in with the rest of the team, okay?*
>
> **You:** *You know I have anxiety and working out front on the registers is not supposed to be part of my duties, right?*

Manager: I just need you for this week, until this sale is over. Can't you just suck it up for one week and be a team player?

You: We spoke about this when I took the job. We agreed that I would help with displays and stocking. You said I wouldn't have to work directly with the public due to my documented anxiety. Maybe you forgot about our conversation. I'll send you a copy of the e-mail.

In this scenario, the employee had secured documentation of their manager's promise not to put them on the registers. The employee reminds their manager of what they agreed upon previously. As the manager continues to pressure the employee into feeling guilty about not being a team player, the employee stands their ground and offers to show the e-mail to support their claim.

A peer or support staff will typically try to cause friction between you and another colleague to take the attention off their role in a workplace problem. This tactic also leaves you with less support. Sometimes they tell you lies about what other people are saying about you, but even if they are telling the truth, they don't intend to be helpful. Your colleague may resent your confidence or how well you do your work and they may intend to make you feel insecure. They will also ask personal questions, under the pretense of trying to help you or get to know you. However, they're usually trying to find out your insecurities. Later, they might use your weaknesses against you. When you don't want to reveal personal information, they may accuse you of being mean or say that your colleagues find you unapproachable. Don't entertain these accusations or show your emotions in front of them.

> **Peer:** *I'm so glad you decided to join our team. You know New York City can be so expensive, but I love it here. Lived here all my life. Are you from New York? Do you live alone? And you're in college, too! How do you pay for it all?*
>
> **You:** *I'm looking forward to helping the team any way I can.*
>
> **Peer:** *I'm just trying to get to know you better, so maybe I can help you out somehow. Plus, the more we know about each other, the closer our team is. I've told you a little bit about me, so why don't you tell me about you? This'll just be between us, of course.*
>
> **You:** *As I said, I'll do everything I can to help the team, but I prefer not to discuss personal topics at work.*

In the previous scenario, the employee's peer asks a series of personal questions under the guise of making their team more close-knit. The employee doesn't answer the question but makes the point that they can still be a team player. When the peer pushes for information, the employee repeats their desire to be a team player while asserting their preference not to talk about their personal business.

> *Support staff: You've probably heard this saying, but it's true: People here smile in your face and then they talk about you right behind your back. They've been talking about you like a dog! I think they dislike you because this is just a temporary job for you, while they feel stuck here.*
>
> *You: I prefer that you don't tell me who is gossiping about me.*
>
> *Support staff: I'm just letting you know what they said, because you should know how they really feel about you. If somebody talked about me, I'd want you to tell me. What's the problem with that?*
>
> *You: Whatever you talk about with colleagues is your business. Going forward, I prefer that you not tell me anything about what other people are saying about me. This way, we can both focus on our work.*

In the previous scenario, the support staff comes to their colleague with gossip about what other people are saying about them. The employee states their preference not to know about gossip. When the support staff pushes and tries to make their colleague feel guilty, their colleague expresses their preferences again and highlights how those preferences are beneficial for both of them.

Setting Boundaries

A major part of setting boundaries with someone who engages in passive-aggressive behavior is documenting your colleague's promises. Pay more attention to what your colleague does, rather than what they say. Written documentation can help prove what your colleague promised to do.

Protecting your emotions is another key part of setting boundaries. People who behave passive-aggressively will often do things to get you riled up or to make you second-guess yourself. Being able to control how you feel about yourself can make you feel more secure.

Yet another key part of setting boundaries is protecting your personal information. Colleagues with passive-aggressive behavior may lie and say they want to get to know you. But once you tell them personal details about your life, they will typically share your information with others. They usually also use this information against you at your most vulnerable moments.

♦ **Get documentation in writing.** For example, you may send an e-mail saying, "To confirm our discussion about my schedule, you want me to work 2:00 p.m. to 10:00 p.m. Monday–Thursday next week." These colleagues thrive on confusion and chaos, and they may try to ruin your reputation by verbally giving you incorrect information.

♦ **Protect your personal space.** Don't feel pressured to hug colleagues or let them stand too close to you. If someone steps into your space and makes you feel uncomfortable, you can move to readjust the space to a comfortable distance. If someone reaches out to touch or hug you, hold up your hand to signal them to stop.

♦ **Avoid meeting with colleagues alone.** They often use this opportunity to treat you harshly when there are no witnesses around who can substantiate your claims.

- **Keep interactions short.** The longer you engage in conversation, the more time they have to make negative comments and ask personal questions. By limiting the time you spend with these colleagues, you protect your energy from being drained by their negativity.

- **Don't go overboard trying to prove yourself.** These colleagues are often insecure and have a hard time admitting when someone is doing a good job. For many of them, nothing you do will ever be good enough, so it is wise not to work too hard trying to impress them.

- **Keep personal information private.** Keep conversations focused on work. These coworkers often come on strong and may do favors for you in the beginning to gain your trust. Then the moment they feel slighted, they can turn on you without hesitation.

- **Monitor your reactions.** Don't show that you're bothered by the dramatic situations they create. Be prepared for them to continue to escalate the situation to get a response out of you, and do your best to remain calm.

If You Remember One Thing . . .

The behavior of a colleague who behaves in a passive-aggressive way is often driven by low self-esteem and a fear of rejection. They create chaos for others and put them down to feel more in control of themselves. Document as much as you can in writing; if they are challenged, they are likely to change their story and blame you for being difficult.

Chapter 6

All Ego,
All the Time

Does one of your colleagues usually try to get the upper hand in every interaction? These people are generally abrasive and make it a point to show others how powerful they think they are. On top of this, they are often critical and try to make you feel as if you and your work performance are not good enough. Working with someone like this can be exhausting, since they never seem to be satisfied. You may feel like you are constantly on the defensive.

A colleague like this may have narcissistic personality disorder (NPD). They usually don't like seeing people happy and free of stress, because they are often in a lot of emotional pain. They constantly compare themselves to others and never feel good enough, so they often insult others to feel better about themselves. A qualified mental health professional is the only one who can diagnose someone with a personality disorder like NPD. However, when you're dealing with a colleague who seems to know exactly how to push your buttons and expects you to put up with it, it's helpful to know some ways to deal with them. You don't have to respond to them with the same mean and spiteful behavior they use with you.

In this chapter, you'll learn how to identify someone who may have NPD and you'll find strategies to help you interact with them. Strengthening communication and boundaries with your colleague involves being aware of your strengths and flaws, realizing when your colleague is twisting reality, and choosing not to give them the reaction they are trying to get out of you.

A Familiar Scene

Christopher is a senior manager of marketing at a publishing house. His department has had a high turnover rate for the past few months. There is a lot of tension in the office and coworkers often look tired, rushed, and frustrated. Christopher constantly criticizes junior managers and loves to e-mail them with negative news right before holidays or weekends to try to ruin their mood. Although Christopher typically makes negative comments about their work, he can never provide the junior managers with specific examples of their errors. Instead of confronting Christopher, the junior managers release their frustration by being harsh with the people they manage.

Christopher uses meetings as a chance to brag. Just the way he enters the room makes his colleagues uneasy; he swaggers into the room and even looks as if his chest is puffed out. He's usually at least 10 minutes late and never apologizes for keeping his team members waiting, yet he publicly criticizes anyone who comes in even a few minutes after him.

At the most recent team meeting, Christopher brags about his weekend activities. He shares that he attended a gala with his brother and mentions at least three times that his brother is an investment banker. He talks about the filet mignon and wine they had at dinner and shows pictures of the celebrities he met. This takes up about 15 minutes of the meeting. However, when other people bring up important topics, he rushes them, stating that there's not enough time to discuss them.

Christopher seems to have targeted a new junior manager, Jennifer. He seems envious of her master's degree and fearful that she may take his job. He never addresses her the way that she prefers to be addressed, saying that she's being too formal. He often makes up nicknames for Jennifer instead or uses a shortened version of her name without asking if it's okay. Christopher doesn't make eye contact with her in team meetings, rarely acknowledges her comments, and makes snide remarks when he does. No one on the team challenges this behavior.

Jennifer's coworkers initially liked her and the work she produced, but now they've started to distance themselves from her.

Jennifer comes out of a private meeting with Christopher one day and seems upset. It turns out that Christopher wants her to help him win accounts in any way possible, even if she must act out of character. Christopher tells her to pay extra attention to her makeup and hair and to wear skirts when she accompanies him to business dinners. When Jennifer attends the next dinner, she doesn't take his suggestions. Christopher appears angry and doesn't introduce her to any colleagues, presents all the work as his own, and doesn't mention Jennifer's contributions.

A few weeks later, Christopher tells Jennifer that she is not doing a good job managing the marketing assistants, although none of the other senior managers have complained and clients have only had positive feedback on her work. Christopher begins to assign her tasks that are impossible to complete so that he can have a reason to fire her.

Christopher then learns that Jennifer is going to quit. He makes her last two weeks almost unbearable, telling her that he's going to make her pay and that he is not going to provide a good reference for her.

Christopher seems oblivious to the problems in his department and figures he just needs to hire better people.

Solving the Problem

Someone with possible NPD, like most people with personality disorders, can be resistant to change and fail to see that their behavior is problematic. If you have to deal with this behavior from a colleague, you may be exhausted and may have even started to doubt yourself.

Colleagues who may have NPD usually study people to find out their insecurities, likes, and dislikes. Later, they will typically use this information to put you at a disadvantage so they can feel more secure with themselves. They will often treat you badly and test you to see how far you'll let them go. The first time they cross your boundaries is a good time to reinforce them. When you must interact with them, keep your personal business to yourself and keep conversations short. Many times, it's best to avoid them if possible.

These colleagues often twist reality, so avoid responding to them in an emotional way, since they feed off that energy. Have a realistic idea of your own strengths and weaknesses and seek reliable feedback from someone you trust.

Colleagues that might have NPD are prone to fits of anger and focus on getting revenge on those who speak out against them. So if you confront them or report them to higher-ups, be prepared for backlash. Finally, have an exit plan just in case things become unbearable.

Dialogue Model

In the following examples, you'll learn how to stand up for yourself when your colleague attempts to demean you. You'll also learn how to handle criticism that doesn't seem constructive.

A manager with possible NPD feeds off making colleagues feel insecure. Their targets are often the nicest and hardest-working people, because these characteristics make them feel threatened. They are uncomfortable with any interaction where their authority and perceived superiority are threatened, and they will quickly try to regain the upper hand. They will often disrespect you by refusing to address you the way you introduce yourself, using a shortened version of your name without asking or by refusing to use your title. They will often make up an excuse, perhaps that they were trying to be friendly, but the fact remains that they imposed a name on you and didn't care enough to find out how you prefer to be addressed. They will also typically criticize the quality of your work, usually without providing specific examples. There is often no real problem with your work, but the person with possible NPD usually has to criticize you to feel better about themselves. They often want to make you feel insecure and see you react negatively so they can feel more in control of their perceived status.

Manager: Jenn. Your presentation needs to be better. Like three times better. You can't show that to clients. What are you trying to do? Make sure we never close any accounts with them again? Get it together, Jenn.

You: I prefer that you call me Jennifer. I really want us to close this account, but what exactly about the presentation needs to be better?

Manager: Calling you "Jennifer" is so formal. Come on, we're all family here. You're telling me you don't know what needs to be fixed? How do you expect to make senior manager? No need to turn this thing into a big deal. Just get it done.

You: As I said, I prefer that you call me Jennifer. I want my presentation to be flawless, but when you say it needs to be better, I need to know exactly what you find problematic. It would also help to know what did work. That way, we can close this account.

The manager in the previous scenario doesn't show respect for how Jennifer would like to be addressed. He calls her by a nickname twice and tries to make her feel bad when she tells him what she prefers to be called. However, Jennifer repeats her preferences each time she is called by a nickname.

She also asks for specific feedback when her manager criticizes her presentation.

A peer with possible NPD will often try to tell you how you can do your job better. They will offer unsolicited advice and act as if they know best and that, if you listen to them, you'll be better off. However, the way they interact with you often comes across as intrusive and condescending.

> *Peer:* *How do you expect the assistants to listen to you? You're too nice to them.*
>
> *You:* *I don't know what you mean.*
>
> *Peer:* *I'm just saying. My father is a Fortune 500 CEO. He was profiled last year. And he says that being feared is more important than being respected. Listen to me: Make them fear you. You control them. Most of them are fresh out of college, hungry for their big break. They'll do anything you tell them to do.*
>
> *You:* *I prefer to be collaborative in the way I manage my team.*

In the previous scenario, the peer offers unsolicited advice under the guise of trying to help their colleague. The peer references their father's high-status job as a reason they should be trusted to give management advice. The peer's colleague does not show offense at the comments critiquing their management skills. Instead, they tell the peer how they prefer to lead, without dictating how their peer should manage their staff.

Support staff with possible NPD are often insecure and jealous and don't like serving those they feel are in a higher position than they are. They will often make snide remarks to make themselves feel better.

> *Support staff: Hey, sweetie, your client just called. They moved the appointment to 11:00 a.m. You, with clients of your own. That's something. Can't believe they trust someone so young to deal with these clients. I must be getting old.*

> *You: I prefer that you call me David, not "sweetie." I'd also prefer you keep your opinions about my age and my work to yourself.*

> *Support staff: I've seen a lot, and most of these clients are cutthroat. They go right for the jugular if you're not careful. I was just trying to warn you.*

> *You: Again, that's your opinion. But I'd prefer that you don't share your opinions with me going forward.*

In the previous scenario, when the support staff doesn't call David by name, he addresses the issue right away. He also states how he'd prefer his colleague to interact with him in the future. This sets the tone for future interactions, and he can always refer to this conversation if his colleague claims they forgot.

Setting Boundaries

Setting boundaries with a colleague that might have NPD involves knowing your strengths and weaknesses. People who might have this personality disorder enjoy seeing you squirm when they pick at your insecurities. When you know who you are and feel secure with yourself, it's hard for them to shake your confidence.

Another aspect of setting boundaries is realizing when your colleague is twisting reality. Your colleague can lie so much that they start to believe the lies they've told you. They may also purposely give you false information just to mess with you.

A final part of setting boundaries is refraining from displaying strong emotional reactions in front of your colleague. They tend to gain their sense of self-worth from putting others down and provoking them, so even negative attention is considered better than none.

♦ **Follow up conversations with an e-mail.** Create a paper trail in case you need it later to help prove your version of events to higher-ups. Even if your colleague never responds to your e-mail, this may show that they didn't care enough to respond, ultimately saying more about them than it does about you.

♦ **Ask for specific examples.** If your work is criticized, ask for specific examples of what is wrong with it. Your colleague might try to convince you that you're doing a poor job even when that's not the case. They often feel more powerful when they can get you to doubt yourself, typically smirking when this happens. In extreme cases, they will literally laugh out loud in someone's face. Many of them have learned to enjoy seeing other people hurt and vulnerable, often due to lack of empathy.

♦ **State how you prefer to be addressed.** If your colleague fails to address you the way you prefer, correct them the first time. You may have to repeat yourself as they will often pretend they forgot what you previously spoke to them about. People with NPD often don't respect others. They may intentionally mispronounce your name or refuse to acknowledge any titles you use, such as "Ms." or "Dr."

♦ **Avoid getting caught in the middle.** Your colleague may pit team members against one another. They will often spread lies about you to other colleagues to paint you in a negative light while lying to you that your colleagues spoke negatively about you. The goal is to isolate you from other colleagues and them from you, so no one has any support. Another effect may be that few colleagues will believe your side of the story.

♦ **Keep personal information to yourself.** Although you may think sharing information about yourself is harmless small talk, the information you share could be used to hurt you later.

♦ **Avoid meeting alone.** Try to meet your colleague only when other people are present. They can get angry when they think you're criticizing them or when they can't get their way. When this happens, their behavior can become abusive.

♦ **Know who you are.** Be honest with yourself about your flaws and strengths, so they can't be used against you.

If You Remember One Thing . . .

Colleagues with possible NPD often put others down to make themselves feel better. Don't let them feed off your reactions or let their way of interacting with you change what you think about yourself.

Chapter 7

More Workplace Difficulties

The behavior of people at your workplace may sometimes annoy or upset you. Maybe they don't seem to trust you, check in constantly to see how your project is going, or never seem to do their share of the work. These types of behaviors may lead to a toxic work environment but are not necessarily caused by a mental disorder.

In this chapter, you'll find some helpful tips for dealing with three types of people whose behavior can make work unpleasant for you. The first is the colleague who micromanages. You may recognize them by their need to control almost every aspect of how you do your job. Another challenging type of coworker is someone who won't accept new responsibilities. They are usually comfortable keeping their routine, and change makes them anxious. You may also have to interact with a colleague who pushes their work off on you. This person tries to make their job easier without consideration for the impact of their behavior on you.

The Micromanager

Does it seem like one of your colleagues is always standing over your shoulder making sure you get things just right? You're probably frustrated by their constant questioning, and you may even be doubting yourself. Not everyone who micromanages has a mental disorder, but if they do, they most likely have obsessive-compulsive personality disorder (OCPD) or an anxiety disorder.

Margaret is a high school principal with a reputation for being overinvolved with the way her teachers run their classrooms. This year has been very stressful for many teachers. During a meeting one month, the music teacher suggests a fundraising campaign. He has a goal of raising $10,000 in six months and wants to use the funds to buy instruments. Margaret hesitates to approve the campaign although most other teachers are excited about the idea. She asks many questions about what could go wrong but eventually approves.

Instead of letting the teachers run the campaign themselves, Margaret is intrusive. She dictates the letters and e-mails announcing the campaign almost word for word and even offers to write them herself. She also tells teachers she wants all money donated through means other than online to be reported to her as it comes in instead of in a report at the end of each week. This means the teachers must take time out of their schedules each day to report any money raised. She visits each class daily, asking how the fundraising is going.

Margaret has no musical training but visits the chorus rehearsals run by the music teacher and gives directions. She suggests where certain students should stand so that it will sound better when they sing, and she asks the teacher if he can make certain parts of the songs sound more upbeat.

The school librarian is also frustrated with Margaret's behavior. Margaret visits the library several times in a week, then tells the librarian to order more print magazine subscriptions. When the librarian tells Margaret that few students read print magazines, she insists they will if they are available.

Margaret is also concerned about making sure more students pass the exit exams that measure their achievement in certain subjects. She sits in on each class several times a week to make sure the teachers are preparing their students the way she would like. The teachers feel smothered by this behavior. Margaret also wants the teachers to have their students report how much time they spend studying each night. She has offered to teach review courses herself, even if it means she will need to arrive at work earlier than usual, stay later, and have fewer weekends off. The students seem curious about her presence, and the teachers start to feel less confident about their abilities. After so many visits to the classroom, students wonder why the principal is in their class so often, and they question whether their teacher is qualified to help them pass the exams.

Margaret doesn't understand why her teachers look like they want to run the other way when she approaches them. It puzzles her that her staff can't seem to understand how hard she works for the school, the students, and her teachers.

Solving the Problem

Someone who micromanages is usually a boss but could be a peer or a member of the support staff. Working with a colleague who micromanages involves creating realistic timelines and setting aside time to check in at reasonable intervals. The key is to do these things before a project begins so that everyone knows what to expect. Timelines can help keep everyone on track.

Your coworker may continue to ask for frequent updates, so before you begin a project, decide how often you want to check in and how you prefer to do it. Will you check in once a day or once a week? In person or by e-mail? These check-ins are also a good time to address issues if your colleague continues to micromanage.

A person who micromanages is often driven by anxiety about being responsible for the poor work of others, so it's a good idea to have a process for measuring how well you completed any assigned tasks. A quality assurance measure—like a checklist of completed milestones—could be helpful. You may also ask your boss or other micromanaging colleague to describe to you what a good completed job looks like, so you can reflect those details back to them in the finished product.

Dialogue Model

In the following example, you'll learn how to respond to your colleague's unwelcome check-ins and unsolicited advice. You'll also learn how to agree on reasonable and specific times to check in.

A manager will likely continue to ask for updates and will try to dictate exactly how you do your job.

> *Manager: I know you work hard with your students, but the chorus sounds a little off. You know what would make them sound a lot better?*

> *You: So you have some suggestions? What exactly sounds off to you?*

> *Manager: It just sounds off. The second verse of that song they were just singing seems too low. The students with the lower voices shouldn't sing during that part—only the ones with the lighter*

voices. I know you work hard with them, and you know I'm just trying to help. I'll sit in on your classes tomorrow and stop in on the next rehearsal to make sure they're in shape for the competition.

You: *I understand that in your opinion the second verse sounds too low, but they are singing the parts the way they were intended to be sung. I'd prefer to update you on our progress at the end of every week. We can meet in my office, and I'll have more time to rehearse with the chorus and make sure they're in top form for the regional competition.*

In the previous scenario, the manager attempts to tell their colleague how to direct their own chorus and invites themselves to the teacher's class and rehearsals. The coworker initially asks for specific details about what the manager finds problematic, then acknowledges their right to an opinion. The teacher uses assertive language to state how they prefer to direct their chorus based on their training and expertise in music.

Setting Boundaries

Setting boundaries with someone who microman-ages involves creating balance. It's beneficial to have enough time without frequent interruptions so you can focus on doing a good job. Still, you probably want to engage enough to communicate that you're committed to doing the best job you can.

- **Create timelines.** You and your colleagues are ideally clear on the timeline for the project before you begin. Complex projects may even be broken down into phases. This is the time to raise any issues you anticipate with being able to keep to the timeline. Are the goals too unrealistic? Do you need more support to meet the deadlines?

- **Use quality assurance measures.** Your boss may be concerned about the quality of the work you're producing, but how do you know if you're meeting standards or if your boss is just being extra picky with you and no one else? What if the standards keep changing? Before you start a project, ask how your boss will be able to tell you have done a good job. Ideally, you'll have objective ways to tell, such as a checklist of specific milestones.

- **Designate time to evaluate your progress.** Since you probably want to do the best job possible, you don't want to waste time. Agree on how often you and your colleague will check in on your progress. Decide how you will check in—in person, through e-mail, over the phone, or a combination of those methods.

If You Remember One Thing . . .

People who micromanage are usually insecure about their abilities and project those insecurities onto others. Agree on reasonable times to check in, and use objective measures of quality assurance.

They Won't Take On New Responsibilities

Some people like to stick to a predictable routine in their workplace. You may observe this colleagueas someone who likes to come in, do their work the way they've always done it, and go home. Your colleague may hate change, learning new things, or taking on new challenges. If this is the case, you may feel as if your colleague is not keeping up with industry standards.

These behaviors are not always characteristic of someone with a mental disorder. However, if they are, your colleague may have major depressive disorder, bipolar disorder, an anxiety disorder, or ADHD. They may be so anxious that they fear not being able to handle their job responsibilities. Alternatively, they may be so depressed that they can't bear to learn something new, or they may not be able to focus on another task.

David is a college professor in the business department. He has worked there for a long time and sometimes has difficulty adapting to new policies. He avoided using the Internet for as long as he could, refusing to create a portal for student assignments and communication. He chose to do things the old-fashioned way, even though his colleagues were quick to see the convenience of the online option.

David has run a very small lab for the past few years, taking on a new PhD student only when another student graduates from the program. Most of David's colleagues serve as the dissertation committee chair for two or three students each year. Several students have wanted David as their committee chair, but he is not interested. He also refuses to serve as a committee member.

David's colleagues are puzzled about why he won't do more. Among colleagues, he says that he can't take the pressure of meeting all the deadlines and working under those deadlines for the years it takes a student to complete a dissertation. He doesn't like change, and he knows how long of a commitment this is. He says he'd rather not be bothered with the pressure and would rather put his effort into teaching the courses he's been comfortable teaching for years.

Despite David's slow attempts to adjust to departmental policies, the business department chair likes David's courses and the way he gets the students to connect to the material. The chair suggests that

David create a new finance course of his choosing. David has thought hard about it but can't seem to say yes. Every time the chair asks him about the idea, David is gracious but always comes up with an excuse. At first, he says he doesn't have the time, then he says he's not sure students would be interested.

David enjoys teaching his courses and mentoring a few students. He is honored the chair has asked him to take on new responsibilities but wonders why anything has to change.

Solving the Problem

A person hesitant to take on new responsibilities may fear learning new things or may not have the mental energy to take on new work. When your manager refuses to take on new responsibilities, you may feel uninspired, possibly resulting in low morale. A peer or support staff who refuses to take on new tasks may create more work for you, as supervisors will often reassign work to others who do not say no. When this happens, the quality of your work usually declines because you're overwhelmed.

Finding solutions involves reassessing your hesitant colleague's role, duties, and any misperceptions you or your colleague may have about these. Is your colleague expecting a change in their title or a raise if they take on more responsibilities? Why is it necessary for your colleague to take on new things in the first place? Will there be a transition period? Speak about the benefits of this change for them and the company.

Another part of solving this problem involves figuring out obstacles and how they can be removed. Perhaps your colleague would like to do more but feels overworked and unsupported already. If you're in a management position, you may be able to remove some of these obstacles. For example, you may agree that your colleague can come in at 10:00 a.m. instead of 9:00 a.m., if taking on new responsibilities means they will need to stay late at work.

Dialogue Model

In the following examples, you'll learn how to identify challenges and find solutions to obstacles that may be in the way of your colleague's ability to take on new tasks.

A peer may not want to help you with team work or projects where you need to work together.

Peer: I was thinking about your offer last week to help you run this internship program for the under- graduate students. It's a great idea and I appreciate you asking me, but I just don't think I can do it right now.

You: I really hope you'll think about it some more. You know the chair will only let this go through if I have another professor to help me run it, and you'd be great. It would really help students, especially those applying for graduate school. What would help you say yes?

Peer: *Well, I'd need an increase in pay for the added responsibilities. I would also need to cut one section of the Intro to Business course to have enough time to help you with the internship.*

You: *Okay. Think about it some more. I can meet with you and the chair to show my support for you if you want. You'd be a real asset to the program.*

In this scenario, a professor needs the help of their hesitant colleague to start a business internship program. The professor compliments their colleague, explains why their help is needed, and finds out what the colleague would need to convince them to participate. The professor then offers to support their colleague's requests in a meeting with the chair.

Setting Boundaries

Setting boundaries with someone who has difficulty taking on new responsibilities involves knowing what is within the scope of your professional duties. This is especially important since your colleague's tasks may be reassigned to you. This is common at workplaces with unclear roles and at places where people are expected to pitch in with everything.

Another aspect of setting boundaries involves identifying what may be making your colleague hesitant. This is particularly important if you're in a management position. Once you figure out what's stopping them, it may be easier to help them clear those obstacles.

◆ **Know your role.** Be clear about what your duties are. Realize when someone is asking you to do things outside your scope because a colleague won't do them.

◆ **Negotiate.** If someone else's duties are reassigned to you, ask what you will get in return. Will you get an increase in compensation or a new title?

◆ **Identify and clear obstacles.** Find out what's holding your colleague back. Do they need more support, a lighter workload, or a raise? Maybe the added responsibilities make your colleague uncomfortable. For example, maybe public speaking has always been something they avoided, and they do not want to take on a new role that requires it. After you pinpoint the problem, you can focus on helping your colleague move forward. At the very least, you'll have a better understanding of why they aren't taking on responsibilities.

If You Remember One Thing . . .

A person's inability to take on new tasks is often due to their personal issues or work environment. Try to identify obstacles and remove them when possible, or encourage your colleague to seek help to remove personal obstacles.

Ropes You into Doing Their Work

Is there someone at work who seems to get ahead even though they seem to slack off a lot? Do they intimidate people into doing their work yet take most or all of the credit?

Someone who tries to get you to do their work may not have a mental disorder, but if they do, it is likely that this coworker may have NPD or BPD.

Tiffany is one of two event planners for a large entertainment company. Her manager has trusted her with planning for the premiere of a film that is scheduled for one month away. Her clients want the event to be in an intimate and upscale setting. Tiffany has been given a specific budget to book the venues, entertainment, and photographers for the main event and the after-party. She must also manage the setup and breakdown of the event.

Tiffany is also planning a smaller-scale after-party for an up-and-coming film production company. As she starts to pay more attention to the prestigious event, she falls behind. She asks Melody, a less experienced event planner, to help with the smaller event. This is not part of Melody's duties, as each coordinator is assigned to plan specific events. Tiffany's requests are small at first. She asks Melody's opinion about a venue, then asks her to listen to music to help her narrow down choices for entertainment. Melody is able to help since she considers these small requests and she has the time.

As the premiere date gets closer, Tiffany's requests become larger. She asks Melody to scout out a few venues. When Melody declines, Tiffany asks if instead, she could look over some portfolios to help her choose a photographer. Tiffany promises she will return the favor one day and help Melody when she needs it. She says that this is great experience and she can put well-known brands on her résumé. Melody is busy planning for her own events. She also doesn't feel comfortable with Tiffany's requests and decides not to help her.

Tiffany can't seem to understand why her colleague can't just help her out since they're on the same team.

Solving the Problem

Dealing with someone who tries to get you to do their work requires clarifying roles. This can be harder to do if you work in an environment that has blurred roles or one without written job descriptions. When roles are clear, it's more difficult for a colleague to push their work off on you. This doesn't mean they won't try, though. For example, your manager asks you to onboard a new employee without training you on the tasks or discussing the possibility of a promotion. In a case like this, it's a good idea to stress why it's best to have people doing the jobs they were trained to do, rather than risk having an untrained person take on those duties.

When you are trained for the same tasks as your colleague, focus on how taking on their work will negatively affect your own. For example, you and your coworker may both be researchers in a lab, and they ask you to enter the portion of the data they're supposed to enter. If you take on extra work, you're likely to do a poor job. What would that mean for your reputation and for the reputation of your department or company?

If you have a very difficult boss, you may sometimes have to try to find a compromise. Find a way to secure credit for your work, and try to make sure you're not sacrificing too much of yourself.

Dialogue Model

In the following model, you will learn to clarify roles, express your concerns about taking on extra work, and negotiate with difficult bosses.

A manager may try to get you to do work they are supposed to do. On top of this, they may also take credit for your work.

Manager: I need a photographer for the premiere I was talking to you about.

You: But in the meeting, our client asked you to select the photographer that will capture their brand the way they want it to be portrayed. You told them they could trust you to personally select the photographer.

Manager: I know, but I'm juggling five premieres. You're helping me select the photographer, but I still have the final say. So it's just like I'm selecting the photographer—I just have some help from you. I thought you were a team player.

You: Each of us probably has some photographers in mind already. How about we set aside some time to look at some portfolios and narrow down the selection together? I see how this can be a great opportunity, and I'd like you to let our client know about my contribution to this at the next meeting. I'll follow up with you by e-mail.

In the previous scenario, the manager personally promised to select a photographer for a client, then tries to push the work off on a colleague, who then reminds the manager what they promised to their client. This lets their manager know they are aware this task was not originally assigned to them. The colleague offers a compromise of working together on selecting the photographer, rather than doing it alone. The colleague also secures a way to get credit for their work.

Setting Boundaries

Setting boundaries with a colleague who tries to get you to do their work involves clarifying roles from the start of a project. When the roles are clearly different, highlight the risks of doing a job you're not trained to do. When roles are similar, focus on the impact of extra work on the quality of the work you already have to complete.

Another part of setting boundaries involves making compromises when you're working with a resistant boss or manager. Instead of doing all their work, try to find the middle ground and a way you can benefit from the situation.

♦ **Clarify roles.** From the start of a project, determine who will be responsible for specific tasks and why. You may have to consult your written job description if one was given to you. Focus on how the quality of work and the safety of your consumers or colleagues may be affected if you do a job you're not equipped to handle.

♦ **Find a compromise.** This may be particularly helpful when working with a supervisor or manager who may be more resistant to you speaking up about their behavior. In this case, try to agree to a scenario where you don't have to sacrifice too much of your time or energy. In return, ask for benefits, get credit for your contribution, and document the agreement in writing.

If You Remember One Thing . . .

Taking on the work of a colleague takes away time for your own and relieves them of responsibility. When someone tries to get you to do their work, be clear about differences in roles and emphasize why it's best for safety and quality to focus on your own work. If you do agree to pitch in, clarify roles carefully, make sure there is a benefit to you, and don't sacrifice too much of your time and energy for the sake of others.

Chapter 8

Conclusion

Chances are that several of the scenarios you read in this book were familiar. You may have shaken your head in recognition at some of them, as you thought back to painful times you were yelled at, gossiped about, insulted, manipulated, or expected to meet unrealistic expectations. It may have hurt even more if you didn't have support, needed to leave a valued job, or suffered mental or physical health problems associated with your stressful workplace.

Many workplaces are unfortunately unprepared to handle dysfunctional behavior, and some simply don't care. If you work in a toxic environment, you're probably one of many employees who's had a difficult time getting through to management. Sometimes, even Human Resources may not be as helpful as you'd like—they may be more concerned about protecting the company's interests than the mental health and job security of their employees. This lack of support and even participation in toxic behavior from HR can be a sign for you to start looking for a new job.

Talking about mental health issues may not be accepted in your organizational culture and you may be considered difficult yourself for pointing out problems. If you're in a leadership position, hopefully you have become more familiar with recognizing when the behavior of some people on your staff may be disrupting productivity and team dynamics. Perhaps you've discovered some ways of working more effectively with these individuals for everyone's benefit.

This book was written to help you get through work when you feel stuck and trapped, without ways to deal with your difficult coworkers. Workplaces are staffed with all types of people, none of whom are perfect. There could be many reasons behind their behavior—maybe they didn't get enough sleep or they're not getting along with their loved ones. However, behavior driven by life stressors like these is often temporary. When toxic behaviors are extreme, repetitive, and resistant to change, a mental disorder is a likely cause. This book focused on a range of mental disorders as possible reasons for your coworker's behavior.

Anyone can have a mental disorder at some point in their life—your peer, your boss, the people you manage, maybe even you. But it's important to remember that it's most helpful to focus on toxic behaviors and environments, not "toxic people." No one is easy to get along with all the time. Maybe you even recognized yourself in one of the scenarios. Your coworker can change their behavior, but they must make the personal decision to get professional treatment. Some people don't see a problem with their behavior or a reason to seek help. Many people with mental disorders may take a long time to realize how their behavior affects other people and their own lives. Some may be unfamiliar with how to get care and may fear being stigmatized. Others may be afraid to change. For many different reasons, it can take people with mental disorders a long time to get help.

But what are you supposed to do in the meantime? Low support, rigid working hours, poorly defined roles, a lack of methods to voice concerns, bad communication, and poor management can leave you feeling exhausted. It's no wonder that, in toxic environments like these, your colleague's behavior can lead to your own poor mental and physical health. You may wonder why you must be the one to change, while it seems as if your colleague gets to do whatever they want. After putting up with toxic behavior for so long, you may feel hopeless, angry, depressed, anxious, or resentful.

The suggestions in this book are rooted in evidence-based techniques that focus on the ways you interact with your colleagues. Being assertive in the way you communicate is one way. Setting boundaries is another. But some of your coworkers may not respond well to your assertiveness. In some workplaces, people are not used to their colleagues speaking up and can feel threatened. They may become defensive and even accuse you of being aggressive. Even if this is the result, you still tried to do something to change the toxic workplace. You tried to make things work, but sometimes things just won't work out like you planned.

So, what's next? Please take some time to look at the resources listed in the back of this book for websites and tools you may find helpful. You may assess your situation and realize that the best thing for you to do is to leave your job. In this case, it can be helpful to develop an exit strategy. Consider your skills and experience and whether you want to change jobs or your career.

Maybe this experience is opening your eyes to the negatives associated with your field, and you are thinking about changing careers. Leaving this job could be a chance for you to finally go through with starting a new career. You may even be encouraged to start your own business. You may decide to look for another job while you're working, or you may decide to quit and live off savings for as long as you can. Consider how much money you need to save for living expenses while job searching before you can quit. Reach out to your contacts for leads or advice. Start thinking about people you trust who can give you references. Even if you did excellent work in toxic environments, your boss may retaliate because you spoke out. When this happens, these managers often don't give positive references, and you usually don't find out until you always seem to fall short of being selected for a new job.

Maybe you've decided that you want personalized help and are thinking about contacting a licensed mental health professional, such as a psychologist. If you're still on the job, therapy can help you more specifically address the emotional and practical issues related to your experience. The emotional aspects involve identifying and decreasing negative thoughts and emotions associated with workplace issues. Do you get anxious thinking about all the responsibilities you're expected to handle despite so much dysfunction? Are you angry that you're being treated a certain way? Practical issues involve more of the techniques discussed in this book. How can you be more assertive? How can you set boundaries?

It's also a good idea to get professional help to deal with the aftermath of working in a toxic workplace. Many people feel hurt, ashamed, angry, depressed, and shocked long after they leave a toxic situation. You may blame yourself for how you were treated or find it hard to stop thinking or talking about how awful an experience you had. You may have had such a terrible experience that you avoid starting over at a new job for fear of running into a similar situation. Therapy can help you work through these fears.

Choosing to seek therapy and selecting a therapist are not easy decisions. If you have a primary care physician, a first step may be asking them for a referral. You can also search online directories. In the resources section, I've included a website that can help you locate psychologists. Many therapists offer free phone consultations; these are not therapy sessions but brief conversations to help you and the therapist determine if there is a good fit before scheduling an appointment. Don't be afraid to ask a potential therapist about their experience working with people like yourself who have the problems you do. Facing certain issues in therapy may be hard at times, but the confidence, insight, resilience, and positive behavioral changes you can develop make your hard work worth the effort.

You may also want to recognize signs of a toxic work environment before accepting a new job. Although you won't know the true state of the workplace until you're on the job, you can observe and evaluate. Consider how staff members communicate with you from the time you're contacted for an interview. What is the tone that staff use when speaking to you? Is the communication clear? Do they address you by your preferred name? Are people slow to respond to your e-mails or phone calls? Do their behaviors match their words? If you have an on-site interview, do employees look disgruntled or stressed? Are they hesitant to speak with you about their experiences? Are roles clearly defined? It may also be helpful to find out why the position you're applying for is open and where the previous employee went.

Your experiences may not have been what you expected when you started your job, but even if they weren't pleasant, your experience was not in vain.

Perhaps you can look back on what you learned from working in a toxic environment and use it to make things better for yourself or a colleague in the future. Whether you've decided to stick it out or walk away from your job, you have the power to decide how you're going to react to a toxic situation. My hope is that each day you walk into work, whether at your current job or at future jobs, you will feel prepared to respond to any chaos and dysfunctional behavior from a place of inner strength.

Resources

ADA National Network:
https://www.ADAta.org

Provides information for employers and employees about the rights of people in the workplace with disabilities.

American Psychological Association,
PSYCHOLOGIST LOCATOR:
https://locator.apa.org/

Locate psychologists based on several factors, such as their location and the problems they treat.

Lackey, Shonda, PhD. *Psychological Self-Defense: Strategies to Combat Rude, Inconsiderate, and Disappointing Behavior.*

Learn common motivations for behavior and take charge of how you're treated at work, in your personal relationships, and in everyday life.

Workplace Bullying Institute:
https://www.workplacebullying.org

Provides information for employers on how to identify, address, and prevent workplace bullying. Offers
solutions for employees on how to cope with the
effects of workplace bullying.

References

ADA National Network. "Reasonable Accommodations in the Workplace." Accessed January 9, 2020. https://adata.org/factsheet/reasonable-accommodations-workplace.

ADA National Network. "What Is the Americans with Disabilities Act (ADA)?" Accessed January 9, 2020. https://adata.org/learn-about-ada.

American Psychiatric Association. *Diagnostic and Statistical Manual of Mental Disorders: DSM-5.* Arlington, VA: American Psychiatric Association, 2013.

American Psychiatric Association Foundation Center for Workplace Mental Health. "Workplace Stress." Accessed January 9, 2020. http://www.workplacementalhealth.org/Mental-Health-Topics/Workplace-Stress.

American Psychological Association. "Evidence-Based Practice in Psychology." Accessed January 9, 2020. https://www.apa.org/practice/resources/evidence.

American Psychological Association Center for Organizational Excellence. "Benefits of a Psychologically Healthy Workplace." Accessed January 9,

2020. http://www.apaexcellence.org/resources /creatingahealthyworkplace/benefits.

Mayo Clinic Staff. "Stress Management: Being Assertive: Reduce Stress, Communicate Better." May 9, 2017. https://www.mayoclinic.org/healthy-lifestyle /stress-management/in-depth/assertive/art -20044644.

Mind Tools. "How to Be Assertive. Asking for What You Want Firmly and Fairly." Accessed January 9, 2020. https://www.mindtools.com/pages/article /Assertiveness.htm.

National Alliance on Mental Illness. "Mental Health by the Numbers." Last modified September 2019. https://nami.org/learn-more /mental-health-by-the-numbers.

Selva, Joaquín. "How to Set Healthy Boundaries: 10 Examples + PDF Worksheets." *PositivePsychology.com.* Last modified October 27, 2019. https:// positivepsychology.com/great-self-care-setting -healthy-boundaries/.

Speed, Brittany C., Brandon L. Goldstein, and Marvin R. Goldfried. "Assertiveness Training: A Forgotten Evidence-Based Treatment." *Clinical Psychology: Science and Practice* 25, no. 1 (March 2018): 1–20. doi:10.1111/cpsp.12216.

World Health Organization. "Mental Health in the Workplace." May 2019. https://www.who.int /mental_health/in_the_workplace/en/.

Index

A

Americans with Disabilities
Act (1990), 20
Anxiety disorders, 8–9
assertive communication,
115–116
assertive communication
with, 39–43
boundary setting, 44–46, 116–117
and need for reassurance,
35–36, 38–39, 47
and unwillingness to take
on new responsibilities,
112–115, 118
Assertive communication, 30–32
anxiety disorders, 115–116
attention-deficit/hyperactivity
disorder (ADHD), 115–116
attention-deficit/hyperactivity
disorder (ADHD) and, 67–71
mood disorders, 54–58, 115–116
obsessive-compulsive
personality disorder
(OCPD), 109–110
personality disorders, 82–86,
109–110, 121–122
and workplace conflict, 39–43

Assertiveness, 20, 28–32, 127–128
Attention-deficit/hyperactivity
disorder (ADHD), 16–17
assertive communication, 67–71,
115–116
boundary setting, 71–74, 116–117
and time-management issues,
63–64, 66–67, 75
and unwillingness to take
on new responsibilities,
112–115, 118

B

Beck, Aaron T., 28
Bipolar disorder, 11. *See also*
Mood disorders
Borderline personality disorder
(BPD), 13–14. *See also*
Personality disorders
Boundary setting, 30–32
anxiety disorders, 44–46, 116–117
attention-deficit/hyperactivity
disorder (ADHD), 71–74,
116–117
mood disorders, 58–61, 116–117

Boundary setting *(continued)*
    obsessive-compulsive
        personality disorder
        (OCPD), 110–111
    personality disorders, 86–88,
        110–111, 122–123

C

Career-changing, 128–129
Cognitive behavioral therapy
    (CBT), 27–29

D

Davison, Gerald, 28
Dialogue modeling, 30–31. *See*
    also Assertive communication

E

Egotism
    assertive communication, 96–99
    boundary setting, 100–102
    and narcissistic personality
        disorder (NPD), 91–92,
        95, 103
Ellis, Albert, 28

F

Focus, lack of
    assertive communication, 54–58
    boundary setting, 58–61
    mood disorders and, 49–50,
        53–54, 61

G

Generalized anxiety disorder, 8–9
Goldfried, Marvin, 28–29

I

"I" statements, 30–31

L

Lazarus, Arnold, 28

M

Major depressive disorder, 10. *See*
    also Mood disorders
Mental disorders
    prevalence of, 18–19
    toxic behaviors vs. toxic people,
        5–6, 126–127
    and workplace conflict, 2–5, 7
Micromanagement
    assertive communication,
        109–110
    boundary setting, 110–111
    and obsessive-compulsive
        personality disorder
        (OCPD), 106–109, 112
Mood disorders, 10–11
    assertive communication,
        115–116
    assertive communication
        with, 54–58
    boundary setting, 58–61, 116–117

Mood disorders *(continued)*
and lack of focus, 49–50,
53–54, 61
and unwillingness to take
on new responsibilities,
112–115, 118

N

Narcissistic personality disorder
(NPD), 12–13. *See also*
Personality disorders
assertive communication,
82–86, 96–99
boundary setting, 86–88,
100–102
and egotism, 91–92, 95, 103
and passive-aggressive
behavior, 77–78, 81, 89
Neurodevelopmental
disorders, 16–17

O

Obsessive-compulsive personality
disorder (OCPD), 14–15
assertive communication,
109–110
boundary setting, 110–111
and micromanagement,
106–109, 112

P

Panic disorder, 9
Passive-aggressive behavior
assertive communication, 82–86
boundary setting, 86–88
personality disorders and,
77–78, 81, 89
Personality disorders, 12–15
assertive communication,
82–86, 121–122
boundary setting, 86–88,
122–123
and getting others to do their
work, 118–119, 123
and passive-aggressive
behavior, 77–78, 81, 89
Productivity, 23–24
Professional help, 129–130

R

Reasonable accommodations,
20–21
Reassurance, need for
anxiety disorders and, 35–36,
38–39, 47
assertive communication, 39–43
boundary setting, 44–46

Reassurance, need for *(continued)*
Responsibilities, unwillingness to
    take on new, 112–115, 118
    assertive communication,
        115–116
    boundary setting, 116–117

S

Selva, Joaquín, 31
Social phobia, 9
Stress, 21–23

T

Therapy, 129–130
Time-management issues
    assertive communication, 67–71
    attention-deficit/hyperactivity
        disorder (ADHD) and,
        63–64, 66–67, 75
    boundary setting, 71–74
Toxic behavior, 5–6, 126–127

W

Wolpe, Joseph, 28
Work, getting others to do their
    assertive communication,
        121–122
    boundary setting, 122–123
    personality disorders and,
        118–119, 123
Workplace health, 25–26

About the Author

Shonda Lackey, PhD, earned her doctorate in clinical psychology from St. John's University. Dr. Lackey completed clinical training at various sites including Yale University School of Medicine and New York-Presbyterian. She is a licensed clinical psychologist with over a decade of experience. She can be found online at **DrShondaLackey.wordpress.com**.